WADE A LITTLE DEEPER, DEAR

A WOMAN'S GUIDE TO FLY FISHING

WADE
A LITTLE
DEEPER,
DEAR

A WOMAN'S GUIDE TO FLY FISHING

Gwen Cooper
and
Evelyn Haas

Drawings by Bonnie Laurie Russell

Nick Lyons Books

Lyons & Burford, Publishers

THE CORTLAND LIBRARY

This fine book is one of a continuing series, sponsored by Cortland Line Company, Inc., Cortland, New York, designed for all fly fishermen—from beginning to advanced sportsmen. The series currently includes *Fly Rodding for Bass* by Charles F. Waterman, *Superior Flies* by Leonard M. Wright, Jr., *Practical Salt Water Fly Fishing* by Mark Sosin, and *Wade a Little Deeper, Dear: A Woman's Guide to Fly Fishing* by Gwen Cooper and Evelyn Haas.

© 1979 by California Living Books
Revised edition © 1989 by Gwen Cooper and Evelyn Haas

First printing 1979
Second printing 1980
First revised edition 1989

Printed in the United States of America
10 9 8 7 6 5 4 3 2 1
Library of Congress Cataloging-in-Publication Data

Cooper, Gwen.
    Wade a little deeper, dear/by Gwen Cooper and Evelyn Haas.
        p.   cm.—(Cortland Library)
    "Nick Lyons books."
    Reprint. Originally published: San Francisco, Calif.: San Francisco Examiner, ©1979.
    Includes bibliographical references.
    ISBN 1-55821-045-8: $8.95
    1. Fly fishing. 2. Outdoor recreation for women. I. Haas, Evelyn. II. Title. III. Series: Cortland Library (Series)
SH456.C66   1989
799.1'2—dc20   89-35245
                                                             CIP

To Wally and Joe

*who have patiently lived through the many stages
of this book. They encouraged us and buoyed up
our spirits when the "for-males-only" fishing world
tried to shut us out. Their criticism and technical
help was invaluable. Since they taught us
everything we know about fishing, we gratefully
dedicate this book to them. May it serve as a
reminder of all the wonderful times we had fishing
together.*

Acknowledgments

Our warm thanks and gratitude go to our good friends all over the country who advised, encouraged, and helped us beyond measure. Nick Lyons in New York was our guiding light from the very beginning, and our correspondence with him has been almost as voluminous as the material in this book itself. He shared with us his vast knowledge of both fishing and editing, and he encouraged us all the way. His strong conviction about the need for a woman's primer of fishing was most heartening to us. Jim Russell, now retired and living in Ross, California, was another person who counseled us at the beginning. Technical advice on fishing matters was given by our Oregon friends Don Dill, Mel Norrick, Skip Zapffe, and Bill Pruitt. Phil Wright, Jr., took precious time out from his own book to assist us. We would never have made our deadlines if Bud Johns, Jay Stewart, Lynne Casanova, Rita Guiney, and Susan Owings hadn't given us a hand. Phoebe True, Sister Francis de Sales, Marian Heiskell, T. George Harris, John Lindsay, Carol Luther, John Michael Migel, Ann Eliaser, and Roy Eisenhardt all gave us support when we needed it most.

To all these people and many more, we say warm thanks!

Contents

Preface to the 1989 Edition

Wade a Little Deeper, Dear is now ten years old, a rather ripe age for a little book that was written in a burst of enthusiasm by two friends who share a love for a beautiful sport. That this enthusiasm has touched the lives of many other women is extremely heartening to both of us. The world has changed so much in the decade since we wrote this book (especially the role of women) but what we wrote and how we feel about the great spirit of fly fishing has changed very little. It was a great day when our good friend and mentor, Nick Lyons, agreed to take over the details and publish a third edition.

Happily, the same decade is being celebrated this year by a symposium on catch-and-release fishing called, "A Decade of Experience." The findings at this meeting, hosted by Humboldt State Department of Fisheries, are a wonderful tribute to stream management and conservation programs. Its message is simple, and is one we endorse wholeheartedly: "A healthy wild-fish population makes for happier fishing"—catch a handsome, healthy fish, then return it safely to the water, and both fisherman and fish can brag about the battle, both sides claiming victory.

In this anxious age of perilous politics and gloomy environmental forecasts, it is reassuring to realize that some of the dire prophecies of Rachel Carson are being overturned as men and women, working together, give the world's fish population a chance to sustain itself.

Roger Barnhard and Terry Roelofs, in their report on this symposium (published in *Rod and Reel* Magazine), say that one of the earliest (1958) experiments on the exclusive use of barbless hooks, artificial flies, and catch-and-release methods was held on Young Woman's Creek in Pennsylvania. Whoever that Young Woman was, or is, we hope that she knows that the fish population on her stream increased dramatically after the experiment.

We have not basically changed our initial text except to update the information on equipment, addresses, new theories, and such; here and there we have also been able to add some interesting new material. Chiefly, though, we're very happy that *Wade a Little Deeper, Dear* is back in print and hope that it continues to make friends and enables them to enjoy fishing as much as we have.

GWEN and EVIE

Preface

This book is a genial invitation—and one that's long overdue. It invites women to find their "wilderness" selves, and in particular to become fly fishers.

There has been no fly fishing book by and for women before. Oh, a certain mysterious Dame Juliana wrote a treatise once, back when all this fly fishing started, but that's not a book primarily for women. The distinction is interesting and important. I have heard it argued that there is only *one* fly-fishing world—for anyone, young and old, male or female, who wants to step into its sweet waters—and that books should be for anyone. Ideally, that's so. Ideally.

There have always been a few superb female fishermen (and I bow to the authors' use of that last word, in this book, as a "feminine noun"): the versatile and adroit Joan Wulff is a conspicuous and happy example today. In fact, some women, who have fly fished for many years, on equal terms with men, often superior in skill to the men they fished with, may find the very idea of a book such as this troubling. They'd be wrong. And this book isn't for them. For despite the presence of a handful of female fly fishers, and a handful of clubs for women, the numbers are very low.

I wish this weren't so.

My experience has been that, in most (but not all) cases, the male of the species has acquired the love of the outdoors and of fly fishing first. He has founded his clubs, often to the exclusion of women, and he has developed his particular brand of male camaraderie. Too often, though not always, he has excluded women. He has used his fishing to "get away," as a kind of vestige of the frontier mentality—or he has tried to convert a non-fishing female friend and failed miserably.

I suspect the failure was in the method.

He may have demanded too much too soon; he may have *condescended* to let her try *his* sport. He may have given her *his* books: and most fly-fishing books *are* too technical, and male-oriented, for the female novice.

This book is not written by experts. Evie Haas and Gwen Cooper call themselves "happy addicts," and their book should be read in that spirit. It is for women, chiefly; it is a genial, helpful primer for women who want to take up fly fishing. At times the authors are warm and engaging, as they share privileged trips they've taken to the storied Rogue River in Oregon, New Zealand, and Montana's haunting rivers. At times they are practical and helpful, sharing what they've learned. There is a solid section on the mechanics of fly fishing—casting, fly selection, stream lore, the basic knots—which will serve as an elementary introduction to prospective newcomers; to it is added a plea for stream etiquette and conservation. Reading this section, men may learn why they could not teach a woman with whom they wanted to share their fly-fishing lives; and women will *learn,* for Evie and Gwen are good teachers.

But the authors go further. They discuss the possible perils Pauline will face, and how to prepare for them. They are marvelously detailed in suggesting what to bring and what to stock in a medical kit—and both the perils and preparations are different for women. Size and biology dictate fly fishing capacities for most women, and these issues are present too if backpacking is included in the experience—which it is here. And there is a helpful and valuable chapter on what to do if the fish aren't biting; I've never seen gem-hunting, gold-panning, photography, bird-watching, and nature study included in a fly-fishing book before—and am pleased to see them here, since the sport is in many ways a portal to the wilderness, not an isolated event.

We might have expected a chapter on cooking, and we get an especially good one—filled with both gourmet and more rustic recipes. Quite temptingly, we are introduced to trout cooked "corn-on-the-cob" style, in a Dutch oven, in mint leaves, Chinese style, Teriyaki, salted, smoked, baked, in a variety of delicious sauces, stuffed, grilled, in soups, au Bleu, in salads; and there is a special section on what to do with leftovers. *Leftovers?* These ladies catch enough for that? *I* barely get enough for starters.

Here and there in the annals of fly-fishing, there has been mention of a woman or two, usually at the expense of women. One frightening story describes how a male addict taught his wife to fish and then, to his eternal regret, was last seen carrying *her* creel. I know of several anecdotes—told perhaps by frightened, threatened men—about how competitive women become when roused. I once read John Taintor Foote's *A Wedding Gift* to a woman, barely able to contain my laughter when the poor new wife is taken to the northwoods of Maine on her honeymoon and blunders a brook-trout-netting operation miserably; my listener turned away and said, quite soberly, "That's not funny at all." Mostly what we get in the literature is a parade of patient, long-suffering women, bewildered and misplaced women,

3

and various brands of the fishing widow. I have been guilty of popularizing some of the latter, though my intention was always to suggest that *it shouldn't be so*. I saw a lot of such women once and wished I hadn't. I see fewer lately. And perhaps I've grown just a touch wiser.

I warmly hope that this book will herald a new era. "Role" types have been breaking down for a long time now; "feminine" activities have become available to men, to their increased pleasure; and traditionally "male" activities (why they became "traditionally" so in the first place is another story) are increasingly available to women.

It would be presumptuous for me to welcome women aboard: it's not *my* fly-fishing world; it does not belong to men; and many women are already better fly fishers than some men will ever be. Let's say merely that I'm delighted the wall I've seen for many years is crumbling. The invitation is out. The pleasures of an ever-fascinating sport are available to everyone. Evie and Gwen have contributed to this, and have performed a marvelous service.

Bravo!

—NICK LYONS
November 1979
New York

Fisherman Can Be
A Feminine Noun

1

A lmost every woman has a wilderness self as well as a domestic self, something in her nature that responds to the unexpected beauty of wildflowers, to the mysterious instinct of migratory birds, to the ferocious gentleness of wild mother bears feeding cubs, to the vulnerability of a doe protecting fawns. In becoming fly fishermen we began to cultivate our wilderness selves, realizing for the first time that we are citizens of the earth as well as homemakers and citizens of our communities.

Gwen's Story

I was facing one of the crossroads of my life—a lonely period—when I became seriously interested in the sport of fishing. Joe and I had been married for twenty-two years—years primarily involved with the raising of our two children, Little League, Campfire Girls, P.T.A. meetings, and family vacations. Then, one August week, both children moved away from the family home at the same time, Marky to marry an Englishman and make her new home in Oxford and young Joe to go as a freshman to the University of Oregon.

Joe and I, who had not lived alone together since the first year of our marriage, were suddenly shy with each other and surrounded by silence. Still comparatively young and healthy, we were not yet ready for the pasture or the retirement home. I missed the sound of young music and young voices so I eased my loneliness by working for the Red Cross, taking piano lessons, and attending afternoon symphony concerts. I became obsessed with my love for music. Joe, missing his evenings sitting in the high school bleachers watching his son play baseball and football, began furiously tying flies and reading books from his fishing library. He missed young Joe—son and fishing buddy—and dreamed of going back to Alaska for another crack at the "Big Ones." Obviously, there was a growing gap in the relationship, a gap crossed first by Joe, who said, "Why don't you share some of your music with me? Aren't there any night concerts we could attend together?"

Immediately I exchanged my Thursday afternoon symphony tickets for a pair of seats on Wednesday nights. This proved to be such a delightful companionable experience that we also decided to attend opera performances. Then it was my turn to reach a hand into Joe's world. "How would you like to take me with you on your dream trip to Alaska? Maybe you could teach me to catch a 'Big One'."

Joe, although a bit dubious, set about the task of teaching me to fish. He bought me my first pair of waders, taught me to tie simple knots and took me to the high school football field to learn to fly-cast. Then we went off to Alaska where I caught some "Big Ones" and found my wilderness self!

Evie's Story

"How did you learn to fish?" I was asked. Looking back, I conclude, that like the monk in the commercial says, "It's a miracle!"

I grew up in New York City surrounded by tall buildings and grey asphalt pavements. The out-of-doors consisted of a walk to and from the Paramount or Capital movie theatres every Saturday and Sunday afternoon. Gregory Peck hacking his way through the African jungles to fight the crocodiles was my idea of the wilderness.

As I grew older, I was sent out of the summer heat to a camp in Maine. Here scented pine trees, shimmering lakes, and wildflowers were added to my vista. I learned to paddle a canoe and take long hikes that ended with an ice cream as a reward. Camping trips were special treats although we slept in scratchy army blankets folded and closed with blanket pins resembling giant safety pins. Down sleeping bags were yet to be discovered.

My fishing career finally started when I married Wally. We began exploring the rivers of California on weekends and vacations. Since he was learning his business from the bottom, time off and funds were both modest and limited. Patiently he taught me to cast—a bit at a time. Eventually the fishing began to occasionally produce results and I would catch a small, hungry fish instead of snagging my sleeve, a willow behind me, or the floating log in the water. The next problem was how to kill this wiggly, hyperactive creature. After beaching the fish I would throw stones at him until he stopped flopping about. Then, in order to remove the hook I would wrap the fish in toilet-tissue stored in my back pocket. As Wally followed me down the river he would gather the toilet tissue-fish resting on the rocks. As years went on I eventually learned to kill, unhook, carry, and even clean my own fish properly.

As our children grew up the family went on yearly camping trips in Yosemite, the Sierra, Oregon, Wyoming, and Montana. In order to teach them to fish and have them enjoy the sport we found isolated lakes and rivers where hungry fish cooperated by biting at almost every cast. The happy results were that they too have become hooked on fishing.

Unlikely converts, perhaps, but now we are hopelessly happy addicts to the joys of fly fishing, and this primer is partially a "how to" but essentially a "why to" intended to introduce other women to these joys. And remember that throughout these pages "fisherman" is a feminine noun.

The Literary Stream

lowing through every fisherman's life are two rivers, one where he wets his boots and casts his line and the other river a literary stream that winds around his library shelves and flows across the smooth surfaces of his coffee tables.

Both of these streams are filled with fish, some real and some imaginary. Many fascinating writers have contributed both humor and valuable information to this literary tributary.

Dame Juliana Berners, who scholars of medieval literature say "flourished in the year 1430," is such a dramatic historical figure that one can easily mistake her for the heroine of a romantic novel. Actually, she is the author of the *Treatyse of Fysshynge Wyth an Angle,* one of the earliest English-language instruction books for sport fishermen. Born of a noble British family, Juliana lived during the War of the Roses. Perhaps it was this national rebellion that drove her into a convent, for she became a Benedictine nun, the prioress of a nunnery in Sopwell near the great Norman cathedral of St. Albans.

As with all things related to fishing, a great deal of luck was involved—a chain of fortunate circumstances—that facilitated the writing and publication of her book. The first bit of good fortune was that Juliana was able to read and write—a rare talent for an early fifteenth-century woman. The second was that one of the earliest English printing presses was located right at St. Albans. The treatise stood by itself as a single manuscript, but later (1496) it was included with four other sporting documents under the larger title, *The Book of St. Albans.* The other four treatises are on hunting, hawking, fowling, and heraldry. It is a marvelous compendium of chivalrous instruction for medieval gentlemen.

These days, fly fishing is still considered the sport of gentlemen, maybe because of its chivalrous and formal background. An unwritten code of ethics underlies the whole activity. The fifteenth-century Juliana urges anglers to be careful with other people's property: "I charge you to break no man's hedge in going about sports, nor open any man's gates without shutting

them again." In addition, she admonishes fishermen not to kill more fish than they can eat. Written in simple natural prose, her treatise addresses not only the aristocrat but also "All who are virtuous, gentle and freeborn."

The opening passage reveals the joyous as well as the informative aspect of this treatise:

> Solomon in his proverbs sayeth that a glad spirit maketh a flowering age, that is to say, a fair age and long, and since it is so, I ask this question. "What are the means and causes which lead a man into a merry spirit?" Truly in my best judgement, it seems that they are good sports and honest games . . . and therefore, I will now choose among four good sports and honorable pastimes—to wit, among hunting, hawking, fishing, and fowling. The best, in my simple judgement, is fishing, called angling with a rod and a line and a hook.

It is common knowledge that women in the Middle Ages participated in stag hunts and other "noble pastimes" dedicated to the slaughter of wild animals. Mary Queen of Scots was a splendid equestrienne, riding to the hounds with the gentlemen of her Highland court. The image of delicate ladies, with hooded falcons on their wrists, was woven into old Flemish and French tapestries. Other tapestries portrayed peasant women with baskets full of rabbit-hunting ferrets. But although Juliana was a true medieval sportswoman, she was a solitary and philosophical fisherman. Any woman who has experienced the peace of a quiet morning at the river's edge can empathize with Dame Juliana as she extolls the peripheral joys of fishing:

> . . . And if there are no fish in the water . . . the fisherman has his wholesome and merry walk at his ease, and a sweet smell of the meadow flowers, that make him hungry. He hears the melodious harmony of birds, he sees the young swans, herons, ducks, coots, and many other birds with their brood, which seem to me better than all the noise of hounds, the blast of horns and the clamor of birds that hunters, falconers, and fowlers can produce—and if angler catches fish, surely there is no man merrier than he is in his spirit. . . . Thus have I proved, according to my purpose, that the sport and game of angling is the true means and cause that brings a man into a merry spirit. . . .

This happy beginning then leads into the nitty-gritty details of how to make one's own rods, lines, hooks, and lures. It is a marvelous do-it-yourself book that all fishermen find delightful. Uninhibited by her ecclesiastic affiliation, Juliana hikes up her skirts, converts her walking staff into a fishing rod, and proceeds to outwit large numbers of fish in her local streams. Here are her instructions for making a fishing rod:

> You must cut, between Michaelmas and Candlemas, a fair staff, a fathom and a half long and as thick as your arm of hazel, willow, or aspen and soak it in a hot oven and set it straight. Then let it cool and dry for a month. Then take and tie it tight with a cockshoot cord.

She then makes a hole in the top of the staff and inserts in that a willow wand of the same length. Thus she has a long, strong, flexible rod that can also be used as a walking staff—"and thus you will make yourself a rod so secret that you can walk with it and no one will know what you are going to do."

What a crafty girl she is, with her cleverly disguised fishing rod! No other fisherman can possibly know where she is catching her big fish. In her morning prayers at the nunnery, she asks St. Peter for assistance in filling her creel. Perhaps her artificial flies, assortment of hooks, and lunch are contained within the long, graceful sleeves of her Benedictine habit (the fishing vest had not yet been invented).

All her fishing lines are made out of personally collected white horsetail hairs, braided together for added strength:

> I will tell you with how many hairs you must angle for each kind of fish. For the minnow, with a line of one hair. For the growing Roach, the bleak, the gudgeon, and the ruff a line of two hairs. . . . For the trout, grayling, and barbel with nine hairs. For the great trout with twelve hairs. For the salmon with fifteen hairs.

She then tells her readers how to dye the horse hair to match the water in which they wish to fish:

> . . . and to make a good green color on your hair you must do this. Take a quare of small ale and put it in a little pan and add to it a half a pound of alum and put your hair in it. When it is yellow on the scum, put in your hair with a half a pound of green vitriol, called copperas, beaten to a fine powder, and let it boil a half a mile away. Then let it down and let it cool five or six hours.

Quite a recipe! And then she tells the reader how to make hooks out of tapestry needles:

> You must understand that the subtlest and hardest art in making your tackle is to make your hooks . . . and for small hooks you must make your hooks in this manner, of the smallest square needles of steel that you can find. You must put the square needle in a red charcoal fire till it is of the same color as the fire is. Then take it out and let it cool and you will find it well tempered for filing. Then raise the barb with your knife and make the point sharp. Then temper it again or it will break in the bending.

This creative lady is also the alleged inventor of the first modern artificial trout fly. She describes how to make them from carefully dyed wools and natural bird feathers. John McDonald's book, *The Origins of Angling*, contains some handsome color plates of flies described by Juliana (but tied by a modern-day fly tier, Dwight Webster).

11

Here is a description of her Stone Fly, taken from an early manuscript of Juliana's treatise:

> "The Stone Flye. The body of blacke wull: & yellowe under the tayle and wynges of the drake."

and a May Fly:

> "In the begynnynge of May a good flye. The body roddyd wull and lappid asowte wythe blacke sylke: the wynges of the drake and of redde capons hakyll."

These few comments about and examples from the *Treatyse* are meant both to prick your imagination and show you that angling women have a long and illustrious heritage. Dame Juliana Berners is the forerunner of all ardent fishermen, and is beloved by men and women alike.

Cleopatra, another fascinating woman (better known for her political and romantic abilities), was reported by Plutarch to be just as wily a fisherman as Juliana. Here is a quotation from Plutarch's life of Antony:

He went out one day to angle with Cleopatra and being so unfortunate to catch nothing in the presence of his mistress, he gave secret orders to the fishermen to dive under water and put fishes that had already been taken on his hook; and these he drew so fast that the Egyptian perceived it, but feigning admiration, she told everybody how dextrous Antony was and invited them next day to come and see him again. So, when a number of them had come on board the fishing boats, as soon as he had let down his hook, one of her servants was beforehand with his divers and fixed a *salted* fish from Pontus on his hook. Antony, feeling his line give, drew up the prey and, as may be imagined, great laughter ensued. "Leave," said Cleopatra, "the fishing rod, General, to us poor sovereigns of Pharos and Canopus; your game is cities, provinces, and kingdoms."

Dame Juliana may have been one of the first anglers to put her fishing thoughts on paper, but she certainly wasn't the last. Many anglers are compulsive authors or poets. They pack their pens along with their flies and, as they stand fishing in the river, they are also thinking quotable thoughts. On winter nights, they enjoy reading books written by other fishermen.

Izaak Walton's *Compleat Angler, or The Contemplative Man's Recreation* made its appearance on the English scene in 1653, about two hundred years after Dame Juliana's *Treatyse*. The *Compleat Angler* is written as a dialogue between Piscator, a fisherman, and Venator, a hunter. Much like Juliana, Piscator praises the virtues and pleasures of fishing as he teaches Venator how to fish. Anyone who loves fishing must read about the jolly exploits of these two as they hoist a glass at the tavern to fortify themselves for a merry day on the river. They sing songs, write poetry, and flirt with the milkmaids. Surely this dialogue is one of the best examples of the delightful camaraderie one can experience while fishing with a friend.

Fishermen have many different things to say in their books. Some want to teach—how to tie knots, how to fish "dry," how to fish "wet," how to wade, how to read the water, or how to catch fish. Other books are personal journals. Still others are collections of yarns about "fishin'." One of the most charming accounts of a man's personal experience as a fisherman was written in 1895 by Henry Van Dyke. Written in flowery Victorian English, Van Dyke's *Little Rivers* contains many touching anecdotes about camping and fishing in eastern Canada with his wife, whom he calls "Lady Graygown." She must have been a very courageous woman to brave the mosquito and black-fly infested woods of northern Quebec before the advent of insect repellent and sleeping bags. Maybe she was just mad for the poetic Henry.

Here's Henry, writing about the tent they shared:

It is the most venerable and aristocratic form of human habitation. Abraham and Sarah lived in it, and shared its hospitality with angels. It is exempt from the base tyranny of the plumber, the paper-hanger, and the gas man. It is not immovably bound to one dull spot of earth by the chains of a cellar and a system of water pipes. It has a noble freedom of locomotion. It follows the wishes of its inhabitants and goes with them, a travelling home, as the spirit moves them to explore the wilderness. Another thing to remember is that a family which lives in a tent can never have a skeleton in the closet.

These few excerpts from famous fishing books are only meant to whet your appetite for further reading. Therefore, a list of fishing books and authors is included in the Appendix. Two modern anthologies to start you on your way to becoming the "compleat angleress" are *Fisherman's Bounty* by Nick Lyons, and *The Fishing in Print* by Arnold Gingrich.

Why the Fly in Fly Fishing?

3

W hat in heaven's name are the Professor and Lady Caroline doing in the same room with a Bitch Creek Nymph and a Big Hole Demon? Slumming, perhaps. Why is the Royal Coachman rubbing shoulders with Rat-Faced MacDougall? Are they plotting the overthrow of the Queen of the Waters and the Rio Grande King? Is Jock Scott sitting too close to the Mormon Girl? Strange bedfellows—however, this is not a synopsis of a third-rate mystery thriller. It is a description of the inside of a fly fisherman's precious fly box. The inside is infested with Goofus Bugs, Wooly Worms, Black Gnats, and Girdle Bugs.

These colorful creatures with such intriguing names are just a few of the fly patterns known to and beloved by fly fishermen. But why a fly? A fly

fisherman fishes exclusively with an artificial lure made primarily of fur, hair, feathers, and tinsel, to imitate an insect or a small fish. Although he could probably catch more fish with a worm or a salmon egg, he feels that using a fly gives the fish a sporting chance. After all, angling is a sport—a game—and sport fishermen fish for sport, not because they are hungry or need to make a living. Other means of catching fish *are* available: commercial fishermen use nets; scuba divers use spearguns; deep-sea sport fishermen use live bait; and spin fishermen use metal lures, worms, and salmon eggs. (Some trout and salmon fishermen use worms and salmon eggs with a fly rod, but it is difficult to "cast" a worm without losing it.)

Fly fishermen claim, a bit self-righteously perhaps, that when they fish with a fly they are following a tradition in its purest form. The rules of the game and the etiquette surrounding it have hardly changed since its inception in medieval England. It still has a delightful old-world quality. And even though a fly fisherman may look like an old scarecrow, standing there in the river, inwardly he—infused with the spirit of Izaak Walton—tends to be chivalrous and polite.

Like chess players or ballet dancers, fly fishermen become experts only by mastering accepted classical moves. To a fly fisherman a successfully netted fish compares with the chess player's "checkmate" or the ballerina's final bow. The artificial fly has always been associated with this classical, "pure" image of the fly fisherman. But although Dame Juliana did specify that "Angler must use a rod and a line and a hook," she did not insist that an artificial fly be used exclusively. She does offer advice on how to make copies of May Flies and Stone Flies; but she also tells the angler that the salmon, "which is the goodliest fish," is best caught with a red worm grown in a dunghill. (That's about as déclassé as you can get.)

Because the art of fly tying also had English origins, many of our familiar flies have nice old British names: Royal Coachman, Welshman's Button, Whirling Blue Dun, Hare's Ear, Lady Caroline, Hairwing Highlander, and Jock Scott. As the sport spread from the British Isles to the Eastern Seaboard of the United States and then to the American West, the names of the flies became less distinguished, more graphic. The fine flies of the American continental divide include Joe's Hopper, Goofus Bug, Bitch Creek Nymph, Western Coachman, Grey Wulff, Montana Stone Nymph, Girdle Bug, and Colorado Captain.

Part of the angler's art involves blending the study of live insects with the craft of tying artificial flies. The angling artist creates a fur-and-feather imitation of a live insect on the shank of a fishing hook. Because the principal food supply of the trout is an aquatic insect—probably a May Fly,

Stone Fly, or Caddis Fly—the majority of traditional flies are imitations of the various stages in the development of these insects. The "compleat" angler fishes only with a fly that she has tied herself—but this is really not necessary.

A scientific angler takes the time to familiarize herself with the insects that live in the streams in which she intends to fish. She turns over rocks to look for case worms, nymphs, and other insect larvae, and watches for emerging hatches of flies. A young linguistics professor from Wisconsin, one of the finest fishermen Gwen has ever known, uses his wits and knowledge of stream entomology to catch huge, wary, Labrador brook trout on tiny dry-flies. Fly fishing is attractive not only to linguistics professors but also to scientists, conservationists, philosophers, grandmothers, and others who are interested in a "contemplative" sport.

Fishing is a gambler's game. What other sport has opponents from two different dimensions, opponents that can't even see each other? Imagine playing tennis with an unseen competitor! Ernest Schwiebert, in his book *Matching the Hatch,* says that a fisherman who uses only a dry-fly takes the greatest risk, because this fly rests on the surface of the water. The dry-fly fisherman knows that aquatic insects spend only a small fraction of their lives on the stream's surface; but the charm of watching a wild trout break the surface of the water to take the fly compels the fisherman to seek out this singular delight, exclusively.

The fisherman who uses both wet and dry flies is less of an idealist and more of a realist. This type increases her odds of outwitting the fish by fishing both on and below the surface. Nymphs and wet flies imitate not only aquatic insects in their immature stages but also terrestrials who fall clumsily into the water, as well as insects who return to the water to lay their eggs. Because wet flies and nymphs can be seen more easily by the fish, they must be lively, accurate imitations of the insects they represent.

Historically, the big lakes and heavy rivers of the United States, which differ so greatly from the quiet chalk streams of England, presented a new problem to the traditional fly fisherman. A different breed of fish swam in the "new world" waters—big lake trout and char. It was an American woman, a milliner named Carrie G. Stevens, who, in 1924, conceived the idea of tying a bigger fly, which did not imitate an insect at all but a small fish and could be used to attract big fish. Using some of the tools of her milliner's trade, she fashioned a big, bright, streamer fly, then personally went out and caught a huge six-pound, thirteen-ounce brook trout with her own invention! Since 1924, variations of the Carrie Stevens Streamer fly have effectively lured big North American fish.

17

Another woman, Mary Orvis Marbury, has been called the "leading lady of fly fishing." The daughter of Charles F. Orvis, the famous rod maker, Mrs. Marbury recognized that finely tied flies were needed to accompany her father's fine fishing tackle. So she began to tie flies herself. These became so popular with Battenkill River fishermen that in 1883 Mrs. Marbury expanded her operation, hiring and training a group of women to tie beautiful, artistic, effective flies. This was the start of the famous Orvis mail order sporting goods business.

Carrie Stevens, the milliner from Maine, came into Gwen's thoughts one day while she and her husband were out on a small Alaskan lake. They were in a two-man rubber boat, armed with fly rods and streamer flies. A seagull, perched on the top branch of a spruce tree, acted as fish spotter. When this gull saw a school of smolt (young salmon) rising to the surface of the lake, he screamed and dived hungrily into the silver mass of minnows. Other gulls joined him. Joe and Gwen frantically rowed the rubber boat into the crowd of noisy gulls and cast two of Carrie Stevens' streamer flies into the water. To their surprise, the gulls were not the only creatures following the young smolt. Big orange and yellow Arctic char came from the lake's depths to feed on the school of minnows and found themselves caught by streamer flies.

Because a river or a lake is constantly changing, a fly fisherman must change flies accordingly. In her magic fly box is something to match the water's every mood. When the birds tell her that a hatch of insects is emerging, she takes out a dry fly that will dance on the surface—maybe a Blue Dun, a Sofa Pillow, an Adams, a Cahill, a Quill Gordon, or a Hendrickson. She smooths a little silicone on the hackles and wings, then casts it gently to a waiting trout. And when the fish retire to the bottom of the stream, she changes to a wet fly—a Wooly Worm, a March Brown, a Western Coachman, a Montana Stone Nymph, a Girdle Bug, or a Hare's Ear. Or perhaps she'll choose a variation of a streamer fly—a Muddler Minnow, a Gray Ghost, a Welsh Rarebit, or a Yellow Perch.

There is a tremendous number of artificial fly patterns, but you needn't get confused by them. A fly fisherman needs only a small assortment of both wet and dry flies and a few nymphs. All fishermen are—in addition to being scientists, artists, conservationists, philosophers, and sportsmen—a bit mad! They collect flies for sentimental as well as practical reasons. Each fly is a handsome symbol for a fish they caught or hoped to catch.

As Joan Wulff, a champion flycaster, says, "Although fly fishing . . . can be complex, let your enjoyment of it be based on the simple joys of being in beautiful surroundings, the rhythm of fly casting, the occasional sight or touch you have of one of nature's creatures, and the companionship of your husband or friend." And as Juliana, the nun from Sopwell, said, "It will be a true pleasure to see the bright, shining-scaled fishes outwitted by your crafty means."

Welcome to the river, to the wonderful world of fly fishing. Have confidence that you'll find joy in learning this lovely, interesting, many-faceted sport.

The Perils of Pauline

4

D on't let your gentle nature be intimidated by the tales of horror that returning fishermen may tell you. They may insist that the woods are full of bears, snakes, and mosquitoes the size of King Kong; but be skeptical, be a doubting Thomasina, and remember that all fishermen are notorious overstaters.

One story concerns a doctor who, while fishing in the Canadian wilderness, was approached by an excited trapper. The trapper pleaded, "Come quickly, sir, my wife is about to have a baby!" The physician reluctantly followed the anxious man back to his cabin. Sure enough, the heir was imminent, so the doctor washed the good fish smell from his hands and delivered the baby. During the ensuing celebration, the trapper noticed a small set of scales hanging from the doctor's fishing vest and asked if he might borrow it. As he weighed the infant, his eyes widened in amazement and he shouted to his wife, "Good God, Marie, you've given birth to a thirty-pound baby!"

Exaggeration is all part of the grand fishing adventure; and don't think for a moment that the grand adventure is just for he-men and muscular Amazons. You'll be amazed to see how much bigger your own fish becomes when you talk about it later, on cold winter nights.

As with any sport, certain hazards are connected with fishing, but none are so insurmountable as to frighten a woman away from going on a fishing trip. Anyone who does much skiing is certainly aware of the small orthopedic clinics tucked discreetly among the trees at the foot of most major ski slopes. Sailors automatically duck to avoid the swinging boom when the captain shouts, "Ready About!" Golfers prick up their ears when they hear the cry of "Fore!" The primary danger peculiar to fishing has nothing to do with bears and snakes. Rather, it's the possibility of being snagged by someone else's flying fish hook. The handsome fishing guide who rows the boat for two flycasters does not wear that cowboy hat just for looks—he's protecting himself against flying hooks. You should wear a hat too, as well as dark glasses and a long-sleeved jacket while you are fishing near other anglers.

There are two excellent, new, realistic handbooks written by women for the woman who wishes to have a safe, full, wilderness experience. One is *Wild, Wild Woman* by Maggie Nichols, and the other is *Roughing It Easy* by Dian Thomas. *Roughing It Easy* is a complete guide to camping and camp cooking. Dian Thomas is a home economist whose book is full of wonderful recipes and it also has a splendid chapter on first aid. Maggie Nichols, an editor of *Field & Stream,* covers every facet of outdoor activity from the woman's point of view. In her chapter called "Safe and Sound," she has a particularly interesting section on how to cope with irrational fears: fear of the dark, fear of the unseen, fear of the possible calamity. She stresses the importance of remaining calm when stricken with either a real or imagined danger.

The words "challenge," "danger," and "adventure" are all very closely allied; and often the person who goes into the wilderness is actually seeking a bit of peril, a surmountable challenge, and a small adventure. Little boys have traditionally played hooky from school so that they could go fishing

right then, rather than waiting until Saturday. And grownup fishermen rise happily at five A.M. to scuffle about in the dark woods, even though many sensible fish do not rise until noon. Beatrice Cook says in *Till Fish Do Us Part,* "As with all fishermen, the cold grey dawn and I were old acquaintances—I wouldn't say friends—just old acquaintances."

The degree of risk that an angler takes depends on where and how she intends to fish. If she is going to troll from a flat-bottomed boat on a shallow lake, chances are that the only harm that can possibly befall her is a bad case of sunburn and an acute case of boredom. However, if the fishing trip is to be a real wilderness expedition into remote, unpopulated areas, the fisherman should prepare herself for any number of contingencies. All experienced fisherman have personal emergency kits that they keep with their fishing gear, all packed and ready to go. Some of these survival kits are disguised cleverly, giving an angler the casual air of an unconcerned Daniel Boone. An elegant trophy-fishing gentleman from the Bahamas has a first aid kit that's really a complete traveling drugstore.

Minor irritations can be guarded against before they become major discomforts. Because all fishing necessarily takes place out of doors, you must have some means of protecting yourself from various kinds of weather: sunburn lotion (unscented, or it will attract insects), and lightweight shirts, pants, jackets, and hats that can be taken off or put on, according to the temperature. We are continually cautioned by newspaper and magazine articles on the sun's damage to our skin. Each year sunblocks come out with higher and higher numbers for our protection. Golden tans are out and lily-white skin is in!

Insects are a necessary part of a stream environment, but they should be no problem if you protect yourself with repellent (in some wet, wooded areas it is wise to also have a mosquito net for your face and leather gloves for your hands). Robert Traver advises, "By all odds the best fly dope I know—a kind that makes all insects vanish like magic—is a spectacular rise of trout."

Blisters, the backpacker's curse, can be controlled by investing in a well-fitting pair of hiking boots, a tube of disinfectant, lots of moleskin and Bandaids, and plenty of clean socks.

Learn to identify such rash-provoking plants as poison oak, poison ivy, and poison sumac. Wear long pants and long sleeves if such plants are profuse. Wash any exposed area of skin with a strong yellow laundry soap, such as Fels Naptha. A small, cooling tube of calamine lotion will fit in a fishing vest pocket.

If you are allergic to the stings of bees and wasps, bring some antihistamine pills. If you wear prescription glasses, take along an extra pair.

If you are an out-of-shape enthusiast, you may suffer from muscle strain or heat prostration until you get acclimated. An analgesic salve should help you make the adjustment more gracefully.

Much of the adventure connected with fishing is a fabrication of the fisherman's mind, because you don't need to go into the wilderness to go fishing. You must do it out of doors, of course, but the fact is that most fishing in the United States occurs in readily accessible lakes and streams, where all you have to do is get out of your car and walk over to the water. However, if your nomadic soul demands something a bit more dramatic, you can go into a roadless wilderness area, either as a backpacker or, if horses are permitted, with a wrangler and a string of pack animals. If you plan to spend much time as a wilderness fisherman, it is a good idea to take a good first-aid course at your local Red Cross chapter. If you do not attend such a class, at least carry a first-aid manual along.

Before entering an isolated area, check with the forest rangers for campfire permits. They will have current information on trail conditions. Let someone know where you intend to be, and don't go into an uncharted area alone unless you have the experience and woodsmanship of a John Muir or a Jim Bridger. Wilderness camping and fishing is a risky thing to do all by yourself.

Young Joe Cooper, an experienced fisherman and woodsman, says, "The city dweller has difficulty adjusting to a wild environment because he suddenly loses all of his urban landmarks—street signs, stop lights, directional arrows, lights go on and off with the flip of a switch, stoves that can be turned off when the water boils, a door to close during a thunderstorm. He becomes clumsy and frightened when he has to build a fire for food and warmth and sometimes panics when he can't find his way back to his car." So, as an intelligent city person, before you go off to the woods, you'll take some time to become familiar with natural landmarks; to study woodsmanship and trailsmanship; to learn to read a compass; to cook over a fire; to notice in which direction streams are flowing; and to memorize the shapes of certain rocks and trees so that you can use them to retrace your footsteps. Most important of all, you'll learn to respect such powerful natural things as water, fire, and weather.

Demonstrate your respect for water by wearing a life jacket while rafting, kayaking, or canoeing on big rivers. Even if you are an excellent swimmer, wear a flotation jacket. If you do fall into the water, stay calm and head for shore at an angle. This will allow the current to work for you, and you won't tire so quickly. If you are swept downstream, attempt to go feet first to prevent your head from hitting rocks. The current will help rather than hinder you if you get a chance to right yourself. If there's a boat, stay with it if you possibly can. It will float. And never be too proud to wear a life jacket.

When wading in chest-high waders, remember that if you trip and fall, the waders will fill with water, making it hard for you to regain your footing. Some people tie a ski pole to their belts so that it can be used as a wading staff. Be sure to wear a belt around your waders to keep them from filling with water.

Demonstrate your respect for fire by securing a campfire permit (even though it is not always mandatory) and carrying a small axe and shovel. Wear gloves, or use pans with detachable handles, to avoid scalds and burns. If you do get burned, soak the wound in cold water. Always extinguish your campfire completely with water and then with dirt before leaving camp or retiring for the night. Don't build a fire at all if the weather is windy and the woods are dry. Carry a small primus stove for auxiliary cooking.

Demonstrate your respect for weather by realizing that storms and floods can materialize suddenly in mountains and deserts. Know what to do in case of lightning. The U.S. Department of Commerce's National Oceanic and Atmospheric Administration has some excellent advice, relayed here from Maggie Nichols' *Wild, Wild Woman:*

1. Seek shelter. If there are no nearby buildings look for a ditch, a canyon or a clump of trees your height in an open forest area.
2. If caught in the open, stay away from the highest object in the area. If only isolated trees are around, stay down low but far away from trees.
3. Keep away from hilltops, open spaces, metal fences or lines and anything that is elevated and could conduct electricity.
4. If you are in a small boat on the water get to shore as quickly as possible.
5. Do not handle metal objects such as fishing rods, guns, or pack frames.
6. If you are in a car or truck stay there. These are safe.
7. While indoors stay away from open doors and windows, fireplaces, radiators, stoves, metal pipes, sinks and plug-in electrical appliances.

If a person has been struck, use oral resuscitation and cardiac massage.

Demonstrate your respect for the topography of the land; cultivate some trailsmanship while going into the forest, so that you can retrace your steps should you become lost. Always carry a whistle, a compass, some matches in a waterproof container, an energy bar (or little bag of trail mix), and a small flashlight. Notice which direction the streams are running. One of our favorite fishing writers, Robert Traver, has good advice for the lost fisherman: "Keep your chin up and temperature down, and above all use your head before your legs." If you really do get lost in the woods, the wisest course of action is no action at all. Sit still and let somebody find you.

Demonstrate your respect for any wild animals in the area. Let them *know* that you are in their territory; bears, moose, and snakes will not attack a human being unless startled. So make them aware of your presence—wear bells on your belt, carry a can of rattling rocks, beat on a pie tin, or sing in your loudest voice, and you probably won't meet any bears face to face. Keep your food suspended from a high rope tied between two trees to keep marauding bears out of your camp. A Wyoming brown bear once broke into the Haas children's tent, looking for their supply of chewing gum. Luckily, the children were out at the time—but the bear left the tent looking as though a tornado had hit it.

It is important not to buy the movie/T.V. fantasy that all bears are kind, friendly, Winnie-the-Pooh types. Grizzly and black bears still exist in wilderness areas, and should be respected from a distance. Every year we read of incidents involving bears and careless people. But if you're cautious you needn't fear.

Gwen was once fishing on the Kulik River in Alaska, and suddenly realized that another fisherman was at the far end of her pool. That "other fisherman" was a big Kodiak bear, and behind her were her three brown children. When Gwen saw how close the bears were, she was absolutely paralyzed. Their eyes locked. Joe went down to the boat and started the motor and asked her to stay close to the boat so they could get away quickly if the bear started in their direction. But soon, the humans realized that Mama Bear was not at all interested in them; and, fascinated with her fishing tactics, they remained a safe distance away and watched. First she stood up on her hind legs and looked out over the top of the water. Then she put her whole head under the surface and came up with a salmon in her mouth, which she flung pieces of to her cubs, finishing the rest herself. The entire process was clumsy and noisy, and as long as Gwen and Joe could hear the crunching, grunting, and splashing, they knew that the bears were too busy filling their bellies before going into hibernation to even think about the humans.

If you know that you are going into rattlesnake country, carry a snakebite kit and hope that you won't have to use it. Snakes, like bears, don't deliberately try to attack humans. The wisest precaution against snakes is to watch carefully where you place your hands and feet while climbing up slopes and over rocky walls. But do wear high boots and long pants. If someone in your party should be struck by a rattler, keep the victim quiet, transport her as quickly as possible to a source of medical aid, and immobilize her arm or leg in a lowered position (remembering to keep the bitten area below the level of her heart). Put a loose tourniquet above the wound. Use the snakebite kit only as a last resort (you may have to if you are more than five hours from a source of anti-snake serum). Explicitly follow the directions enclosed with each snakebite kit. There are now on the market pocket-size vacuum pumps that extract the poison from stings and bites.

Yes, Virginia, there *are* such things as snakes and bears. There *are* minor discomforts connected with a wilderness adventure. There *is* a slight possibility that you might fall in the water or break an arm. But please don't be afraid to cultivate and nurture the wilderness part of your soul. Maybe you can persuade that handsome orthopedic surgeon with the snakebite serum to join your next expedition into the woods.

You can even teach him to fish!

Take Only Pictures, Leave Only Footprints

5

Women go gently into the forest. They go peacefully as photographers, artists, naturalists, backpackers, fishermen, and conservationists—not as conquerors. We can be proud of the Margaret Meads, Rachel Carsons, and Jane Goodalls. They have all made their contributions as friends of the wilderness.

To a fisherman, the mountains, rivers, lakes, fir trees, and flowers are an angler's setting. The animals, birds, fish, and insects are her constant companions. It is one ingenious plan where every part depends on the other. Our daily hope is to keep this balance of nature and beauty for future generations.

Dame Juliana Berners warned anglers, "You must not be too greedy in catching your said game [fish] as in taking too much at one time. . . . When you have a sufficient mess, you should covet no more at that time."

The fishing world is working hard for the preservation of our disappearing fish. The slogan of one fishing conservation club—the Theodore Gordon Fly Fishers—is appropriate to today's crowded streams: "Limit your kill; don't kill your limit." The "catch and release" method is becoming more and more popular with all kinds of fishermen. It has worked well on the Middle Fork of the Salmon, where all fish, except injured ones, are released. Traffic there during July and August increases yearly, and strong conservation measures are essential to save this beautiful river, which has been made even more popular by the Carter family's visit.

On such rivers as the McKenzie in Oregon, you must return all large fish and limit your daily quota. In California, there are rivers that are for fly fishing only. On most rivers, you may fish any way you want—with bait, spinners, or lures. But when a stream is restricted to fly fishing only, you have a healthier fish population and a cleaner river. Bait fishing is forbidden on the Deschutes River in Oregon. Only artificial lures are permitted; the limit on the number of fish killed has been reduced; motor boats are forbidden on certain parts of the river; and no fishing from boats is allowed.

Idaho can boast that the Middle Fork of the Salmon River has been brought back to rewarding fishing by a strict catch-and-release rule.

Montana's Madison River and Rock Creek (near Missoula) can also brag of improved catch in numbers and size.

The Big Horn River in Montana, which flows through an Indian reservation and has been opened to the public since 1981, is starting to lose its high quality as too many fish are being killed. The fish run smaller and the rainbows are outnumbered by the browns.

Also affected is the Rogue River in southern Oregon where the quality of fishing has notably deteriorated. In the past few years it has been greatly overfished and the take-out limit per person is too high. There are days when the Rogue looks more like a freeway than a wilderness river.

The Truckee River in California has also gone downhill due to overfishing and vacationers floating down the river in tubes and rafts.

Unfortunately, one still finds rivers throughout the country where there is no control, and the condition of these is going downhill quickly.

Montana's Department of Fish and Game issues the following advice to its fishermen:

PUT THEM BACK ALIVE. . . .
   The following steps will insure that a released fish has the best chance for survival:
1. Play fish as rapidly as possible—do not play to total exhaustion.
2. Keep fish in water as much as possible when handling and removing hook.
3. Remove hook gently—do not squeeze fish or put fingers in gills.
4. If deeply hooked—cut line—do not pull hook out.
5. Release fish only after its equilibrium is maintained. If necessary gently hold fish facing upstream and move fish slowly back and forth.
6. Release fish in quiet water.

If you are a family of fishermen, a good rule is to keep only those fish you can eat or give away to a friend who will appreciate them. And by all means, put back the small ones for next year's catch.

How many fishermen do you know who eat the fish they catch? Ed Zern claims that "roughly two-thirds of all fishermen never eat fish. Fish is brain food. People who eat fish have large, well-developed brains. People with large, well-developed brains don't fish."

Have you ever considered fishing a large ego trip? Why should one want to have more fish in the creel than her companion up or down the stream? Truthfully, angling often brings out both the best and the worst in people. Someone you've known all your life will suddenly, once she has a rod in her hand, become greedy, highly competitive, impatient, or intolerant. But other fishermen are helpful, patient, and full of encouragement. Phil Wright compares fishing to making love. The novice, he says, is only interested in number or quantity. The intermediate angler wants size above all else. And the expert searches for the most unobtainable, crafty, and difficult fish.

When a novice fisherman catchers her first fish, anything can happen! Our friend Margaret left the first fish she ever caught for her husband to clean. She was looking forward to being photographed, her rod in one hand and her intact (but gutted) fish in the other. But meanwhile, her husband unthinkingly let the guide skin the fish entirely, in order to show him how to do it. Accordingly, the guide chopped off the fish's head and tail and removed its skin. When Margaret proudly returned to her cabin, she wanted to show her companions her first catch. But when she saw the headless, tailless, skinless remains of her fish, she let out a scream and began to cry. To this day, her husband hasn't heard the end of it!

A new idea, which is gaining popularity, is to photograph your catch

29

quickly and then release it. The inexpensive Polaroid cameras on the market allow you to do this easily. Then, at the happy hour, you can show your friends vivid proof of your river triumphs—and at the same time give someone else a chance at the same fish. New at your camera shops are pocket-size, waterproof, self-focusing cameras that fit conveniently in your fishing vest. The pictures of your catch won't be ready by cocktail time but they will be fine additions to your wallet or photo album.

Look into such 35s as the Canon As-6, Vivatar Trek 50, Fuji HDM, Minolta Weatheramatic Duel 35, Nikon Action Touch, and Olympus Infinity. The Olympus is the only camera of this group that is not completely waterproof. It does, however, withstand rain or splashes. At a time when photography has replaced taxidermy, these small cameras are the answer!

The Gladdings International Sport Fishing Museum in South Otselic, N.Y. sponsored a Tall Tales Contest as a form of promoting sports fishing conservation. A recent (sexist) winner told of a man who could not get a huge rainbow trout that was lying in a deep pool to bite anything that had a hook hidden inside it. Finally, he used his wife's baked beans as bait. The trout snatched them up, and the man baited his hook with a Rolaids tablet—and caught his prize!

How much this contest will really do to advance conservation is an interesting question. But conservation is worth advancing, and in the Appendix we have listed many conservation groups. If you feel the desire to join one of these, your reward would be your own part in helping to preserve the wilderness—for your own sake as well as that of others.

A cardinal rule of the stream is to keep the rivers clean by picking up any litter you may find along the banks and by never throwing anything in the water. Won't it be a joy to float down a river and not see old tires, beverage cans, and styrofoam cups? The Sierra Club faithfully sends cleanup crews over mountain trails at the end of each season. Trout Unlimited and Levi's have successfully launched a "Bring Back a Limit of Litter" campaign, providing mesh bags for environmentally responsible anglers. Oregon has led the country in setting a good example towards becoming litter-free, but many places still have a long way to go.

World Wildlife and Trout Unlimited are among the organizations working to preserve endangered plants, birds, fish, and animals.

If, as fishermen, we can respect and recognize the rights of others, we all will be on the way to a better world. Above all, the quality of life is more important than the quantity. Take heart, Dame Juliana—your advice is being heard!

Come Join Us!

6

For some strange reason, most American men think that they are born with instinctive abilities to catch fish and to play poker. Perhaps they have been programmed to think of themselves as grownup Tom Sawyers and natural heirs of Bret Harte's poker-playing frontiersmen. A man who wouldn't dream of stepping out on a tennis court to play a few sets of tennis without first taking some lessons from a pro will often wade out into deep rivers, confident of catching big fish, when he has never held a rod in his hand before.

American women, on the other hand, are apt to think that fly fishing and poker are men's games that a woman can never master. But fly fishing is a sport, just like tennis and golf; and all sports have rules and techniques that one must follow in order to become successful. *Any* well-coordinated man or woman, assisted by a good instructor, can learn to be a fly fisherman. If a woman is proficient in some other sport that also demands coordination—for instance, tennis, golf, or skiing—she will have an advantage in learning to fish.

Sparse Grey Hackle, author of *Fishless Days, Angling Nights,* in dedicating his book to his wife, Louise Brewster Miller, declared that fly fishing is more a woman's game than a man's, that women have "dexterity and good coordination, fast, well-controlled reflexes, a light sensitive touch, keen eyesight, and close concentration." So if you are a reasonably agile woman who loves the outdoors and desires to become a fly fisherman, get some instruction from a patient fly-fishing friend, a community fishing program, or a commercial fly-fishing school.

Marion, a good tennis player, is ambidextrous—so when she developed "tennis elbow" while learning to cast a fly, she was able to shift her rod to her left hand and continue her lesson. Since her tennis expertise gave her a good sense of timing, she had no difficulty in mastering this new sport. And Carlos, whose only fishing experience had been with a spinning outfit, was able to catch big trout on a fly in a Montana river after three intensive days of training at the Fenwick Fly Fishing School.

Fly fishing is a sport that knows no age limits. Both children and adults enjoy it. There's no need to "hang up your rod" when you reach your fifties or sixties. Age is no more an obstacle for a fly fisherman than for a symphony conductor. Mary Rentschler, a wonderful eighty-plus-year-old woman from Connecticut, fished the Big Hole River in Montana every summer. Not only did she catch fish, she caught "big fish"! Many retired couples in their sixties and seventies pack their cars with fishing gear and spend weeks exploring the great rivers of the United States. They enjoy the sport—but, more, they enjoy it together.

This chapter deals with only the fundamentals of fly fishing, assuming that you want to start at the beginning. This is important—it would be just as foolish (and frightening) to start your fishing career by wading into a swift, difficult river as it would be to ride a ski lift to the top of a steep hill or mountain without knowing how to get down again.

Simply stated, the angler's intention is to lure a fish to the angle of her hook so that the fish can be pulled out of the water. A fly fisherman uses a flexible rod made of cane, fiberglass, or graphite (not a pole, please), and a hook that has an artificial fly formed on its shank. Bait fishermen attach a worm, live insect, or salmon egg to a bare hook. A fine fly rod is a beautifully crafted instrument that weighs only a few ounces. Fishermen sometimes develop such a possessive love for their fly rods that perhaps only a wife—or a husband who is also an angler can understand it. In *Going Fishing,* Negley Farson attests to his love: "I love rods, I suppose, with the same passion that a carpenter, a violinist, or a Monaco pigeon shot love their implements. I love using them . . ." "I love rods because of their associations, the places they have brought me to. They have been part of my kit, when I travel, for many years. This magic wand has revealed to me some of the loveliest places on earth."

First, on the way to acquiring such love, you must learn how to assemble your equipment. Because of its length (seven and a half to nine feet), a fly rod usually comes in two sections, a butt and a tip end. Some compact rods used for backpacking break down into four sections.

To begin, insert the tip end of the rod into the butt section so that the guides are all in a straight line. Next, secure the reel containing your line and leader tightly onto the rod seat, the line emerging from the reel on the side farthest from the rod. Now thread the leader, which is attached to the end of your line, through the guides, taking care that you don't miss one (a common mistake). Pull out a few feet of line so you can get ready to tie on a fly.

All fly fishermen are expected to know a few standard knots. These assure you that all lines, leaders, and hooks are tied together securely before you cast your fly to a fish. Lefty Kreh and Mark Sosin have written a marvelous knot-tying manual, *Practical Fishing Knots,* which makes knot tying seem simple.

The improved clinch knot or a turle knot is customarily used to tie a fly to a leader. (A leader is a transparent piece of strong, tapered nylon or similar material, about nine feet long. It is virtually invisible in the water.) Every time a fisherman wants to change her fly, she snips it off the leader and ties on the new fly. Wet the knot before giving the final pull.

A barrel, or blood, knot is used to tie a lighter piece of leader material onto a heavier piece to make a tapered leader. During a long day's fishing, a fisherman's leader becomes shorter and shorter as she changes flies. A new fine tip can be tied onto the heavy remaining stub with a barrel knot.

The surgeon's knot is considered by many as a simpler knot when attaching a leader to your line or a tippet to the leader. It's faster and more reliable.

A nail knot is sometimes used to tie the fishing line onto the leader. Some fishermen prefer using two loop knots, one on the line and one on the leader. You can buy leaders with pre-tied loops. We'll have more to say on this subject, plus diagrams, in "Notes About Knots."

Usually, if you are a beginning fisherman, you will fish along with an experienced friend or instructor, who will tie the necessary knots joining line and leader for you. But one glorious day, you will become a self-sufficient fly fisherman, and you'll catch a "big fish" with a line and leader that you've tied together yourself.

Casting is the part of fly fishing that makes the beginner feel awkward and inadequate. However, if you have a good sense of timing, you and the flexible rod will soon make peace; you'll be able to adjust your arm and wrist movements to its supple feel. It is the weight of the line moving back and forth that makes the rod flex, and this flexibility gives you the power you need to propel the fly out across the water. Women *can* do it; indeed, some of the finest flycasters in the country are women. Joan Wulff is a champion flycaster. And one of the casting instructors at the Fenwick Fly Fishing School is a tiny woman who, although an excellent caster, has no desire to catch fish. Some people stop their fishing instruction at this point and train to become tournament flycasters—a fine sport in itself.

As a beginning flycaster, you can learn a lot from a good instruction manual, such as the one put out by Scientific Anglers. But manuals alone won't do it—you really need personal instruction from a friend or teacher. Having an experienced fisherman hold onto your rod with you and direct your arm through the motions of a cast will do more for your timing than all the books in the world. In practicing, you'll need plenty of room; so if you don't live near a lake or a river, go to a golf course, a football field, or a neighbor's swimming pool (making sure, of course, that all shrubs, trees, cats, dogs, children, and relatives are well out of range of your flying hook). And be prepared to receive a few snide remarks. When Gwen was learning to cast on the high school football field, a passerby stopped to remark how few trout there were on the fifty-yard line.

To make a basic forward and back cast, keep your casting arm close to your body, holding the rod handle with your thumb extended along the back of the rod, opposite the reel. Wrap your fingers around the handle to keep the rod steady. Let out about twenty feet of line and have somebody place it on the ground in front of you, in a straight line. Then lift the rod to cause a pick-up of the fly. Next, snap the rod in a quick, sharp, upright motion to force the line to swing behind you, full length. The rod should go no farther back than the one o'clock position (the line must remain up in the air and not drop to the ground behind you). Now wait a moment so that the line has time to straighten out; then pull a bend in the rod strong enough to shoot the line forward (when the line is behind the angler it's called a back cast). Now execute the forward cast with a quick snap, stopping the rod in front of

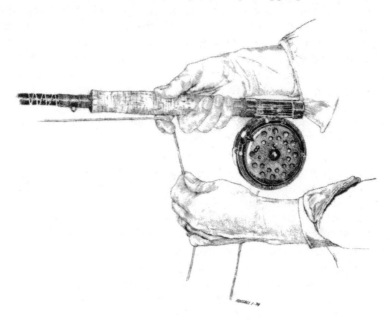

you no lower than the eleven o'clock position. The line will shoot out and your fly will land on the water. If the line lands on the water before the fly or with a fish-scaring splash, try to control the next cast by aiming for an imaginary spot about two feet above the water's surface. The fly will land quietly right where you want it to be. This maneuver takes practice, so don't be discouraged. Stick with the two P's: Patience and Practice. In *A Primer of Fly Fishing,* Roderick Haig-Brown suggests that beginning flycasters who practice in their backyards (or anywhere else away from the water) use a series of six-inch cereal bowls to help them cast for accuracy. If you decide to try this, place the bowls at various distances and try to drop the fly gently into each bowl so that it won't pop out again. If you can accomplish this feat, you'll also be able to place a fly in the water in front of a fish without a splash, and the fish will never know it's there—until it's too late.

Keep in mind the four steps in making a forward cast:

1. Take up the slack line by raising the rod. This will bring the fly to the surface.
2. Snap the rod up overhead, but not back.
3. Pause so the line can straighten out behind you.
4. Snap the line forward out over the water.

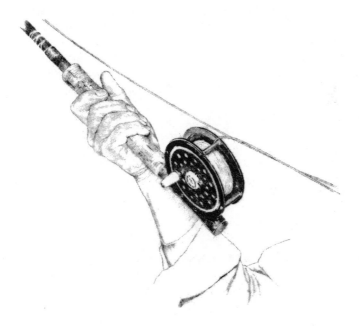

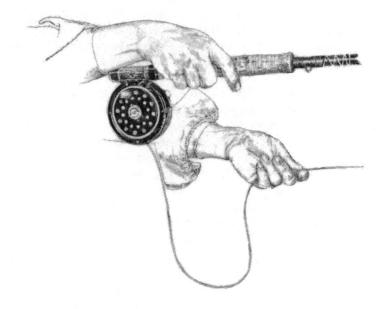

If your motion makes you feel like you're cracking a circus whip, you are using too much power and your timing is wrong. Use your left hand to "strip," or pull, some line out from the reel. Strip out an arm's length at a time. Between casts retrieve, or take in, the line. Move your left hand slightly to pull a few inches of line through the guides—this helps keep the line taut during the back cast. You'll know when you've mastered the motions of casting. As Ron Cordes says in *Flyfishing for Backpackers:*

> With the smooth continuous movement of the fly rod the fly line is lifted cleanly from the water, forming a loop as it rises upward, extending high behind the flycaster for only a brief moment before the forward cast quickly and precisely propels the fly line to a point above the stream where the new loop unfolds, dropping the fly lightly at its destination.

Like many beginners, you will undoubtedly try to see how much line you can cast. But this may cause you to become terribly confused—terribly tangled. Avoid the temptation to show off—stick to the basics at first. Gradually, you will be able to cast a long, lovely line.

Once you've mastered the fundamental overhead forward cast, you will learn the other casts easily. A false cast, used to lengthen your cast or to dry a water-soaked fly, does not touch the water. The forward cast is stopped and a new back cast is started while the fly is still in the air. A roll cast is used when obstacles behind you make it impossible to employ a back cast. A sidearm cast is basically the same as the forward cast except that the action is from side to side instead of forward and back. A backhand cast is a sidearm cast that's made like a tennis player's backhand.

Having mastered the rudiments of flycasting, it is time to put your skill to the test . . . time to catch a fish. There are several different methods of fishing. Sometimes you will fish from a boat. If more than one person is fishing, it can be hazardous to cast while seated in a boat. You need to be extra-cautious with that flying fish hook. Wear glasses, hats, and long-sleeved jackets. On larger rivers, fishing is often done from a boat. One of the most exciting ways to fish is to float down a big western river in a McKenzie River float boat, which is especially designed for flycasting fishermen. It's small and maneuverable in fast water, but it has both a high prow and a stern—where a fisherman can stand and brace herself while casting.

Sometimes, on small streams and lakes where fishable water can be reached by a cast from the shore, a fisherman will walk along a streamside trail and stop to cast a fly into pools and riffles that are close to shore. You may compromise between boat and shore methods by donning waders, with special felt or cleated soles to keep you from slipping, and walking through the shallow water until you are close enough to a fishable spot to cast a fly. The traditional image of a fly fisherman is of a man in waders standing in a river up to his withers, his vest pockets bulging with fly boxes, his net hanging from his shoulder, and a creel strapped under his arm. Usually, he is smoking a pipe and casting a beautiful, long line. If you intend to live out this fantasy, do it—but be careful! Don't wade beyond a safe depth; tie a wading staff to your belt when fishing in rivers with heavy current; and walk sideways through the water, making sure to plant one foot firmly before taking the next step. Wading *is* fun—it makes you feel closer to the fish's world. And your waders will keep you dry and warm, even though you're standing waist-deep in the river.

Now that all the preliminaries are out of the way, it's time to try your hand. You must have a game plan. Fly fishing is a game based on the simple principle that you win if you are smarter than the fish, but you lose if the fish is smarter. Never underestimate the wits of a trout. This fish is slippery, wary, and wily, with reactions like greased lightning. In addition, it always has the advantage of being the "home team." A smart fisherman always makes a plan before casting her first fly. She studies the water, checks the insect life, keeps her shadow off the water, looks for signs of feeding fish, and takes her time. Jim Loudon, a New Zealand guide, showed Evie and Wally how important a good game plan can be. It was a soft warm day on the Whitestone River, a beautiful stream tucked away in the woods. Big fish could be seen resting in the clear water. Jim cautioned the eager fishermen to be calm and warned them that fish are particularly wary in such transparent water. Jim crawled on his hands and knees along the bank so that his shadow would not "spook" the fish. Finally, he told the Haas's which flies to use and which spots to fish. He even advised letting the water rest until later in the day. The poor impatient fishermen did wait, eating a leisurely but anxious lunch before returning to the stream. Finally, by following Jim's advice, Evie not only hooked and landed a seven-pound trout, but also learned firsthand the importance of making a game plan.

You will have to decide whether to use a dry fly or a wet fly. A dry fly, which imitates an insect floating on top of the water, is used to attract fish that are feeding on surface insects. If you see circles on the water's surface, chances are that fish are rising from the bottom to feed. The term "the rise" refers to fish that are rising to the surface to feed. Sometimes you will see a cloud of insects hovering over a particular spot of water. This is called a "hatch" of insects. When a fly fisherman tries to imitate one of these creatures with an artificial fly of her own, it is called "matching the hatch."

A wet fly and a nymph, which imitate insects or insect larvae beneath the water's surface, are used to attract fish that feed under water. There are other flies that do not imitate insects at all; these are called attractor flies. The angler usually moves them in the water. They may imitate small fish or something else that doesn't look like anything to a human but does interest the fish. Normally, attractor flies are used when fish do not appear to be feeding on flies or nymphs; or for non-feeding fish that are going to their spawning grounds.

Next you must look for logical locations in the water in which a fish may be feeding or resting. A fish is usually headed upstream with its nose into the current; but because it doesn't want to battle the current all the time, it normally rests behind rocks, between logs, under banks, or in sheltered back-eddies. Most big fish have a particular spot in the stream, a holding area from which to dart to pick up food. Fish feed below riffles that carry food downstream and into their mouths, or along weedy, brushy banks beside deeper pools. Slick areas that occur where there is a break in the current often shelter big feeding fish. Look for fish in the heads and tails of large, deep pools. These are just a few of the "classic" fishing spots. Unless you are fishing with someone who is thoroughly familiar with the river you're fishing in, stick to the "classic" spots—or you are apt to waste a lot of water, energy, and precious time. Lakes have similar fish-producing areas, frequently in weedy places close to shore or at the mouths of incoming streams.

Once you have found one of these likely spots, cast your fly. If it is a dry fly and you are lucky, you will see a fish rise from the bottom, open its mouth, and snap your fly. You don't even have time to say, "Oh my gracious, what was that?" There's only time to jerk your rod and set the hook. Then, if you can control your excitement, put your rod in your left hand so you can reel in line with your right to take up any slack when you hook the fish (it may run toward you). If the fish runs away from you, let it take line from the reel. Keep an even pressure between you and the fish. Yanking a fish out of the water is called "horsing a fish" and is a no-no. It is not only unstylish but probably will cause you to lose any big fish you hook. The proper sporting way to play a fish is to tire it gradually so that you can lead it, gently, into your waiting net. When the fish is first hooked it will try to get away—it knows the rules of the game and will play to win. Probably, it will jump and try to swim downstream. But be calm. Keep your rod tip up and do not apply too much pressure—the fragile leader will break if you play too rough. If the fish is a big one, you may find yourself saying, "Horrors, I knew I should have retied that stupid blood knot." But relax, the fish will begin to tire from fighting the current and the pressure from your rod. As it weakens, you can slowly reel it toward you. Facing the fish, keep your rod high and pointed in the direction of the fish. When it is a few feet from you, get your net in the water so you can lead the fish into it. Don't thrash at the fish with the net or it will leap in terror, break the leader, and win the game. It is all right to feel like crying if a fish gets away while being netted.

There is an element of mystery in fishing with a wet fly. Unlike the dry fly, the wet fly, when cast, sinks unseen into an unknown dimension where it is prey to all kinds of possibilities. It may get snagged in some weeds, caught under a rock, or be taken by an ugly, sluggish whitefish rather than a handsome brook trout.

Unless the water is extremely clear and calm, a fisherman will not see the fish take the fly under the surface, so she must strike when she feels a tug on her line or sees a suspicious move of her line in the water.

Striking and playing a fish is largely a matter of feel—action and reaction—which is best learned by experience. If you keep your rod tip up and are careful not to let slack in your line, you will improve your chances of landing fish in the process of acquiring that experience. To avoid slack, reel in the excess line. Novices often freeze when a fish is on the line—they forget to release the line and let the fish run. When a fish wants to run, let it. Reels are designed with a drag to keep running fish in check. To get more control, use your thumb and forefinger to put some pressure on the line. When the fish swims toward you, reel in faster. The position of the rod should be no lower than ten o'clock.

"Now, put these all together," suggests Joan Wulff—"balanced tackle, two basic casts, two basic knots, a dozen flies, and felt-soled wading boots, and you're on the edge of adventure! It won't necessarily be easy, but make it your own thing. Take your piece of river and make flies swim or float over every inch of water you can."

There are as many variables to the wonderful game of fly fishing as there are fish in the rivers. We have described just a few basic elements of this fascinating sport. The best way to learn to be a fly fisherman is to go to a river and ask the trout for a few lessons.

7

What to Bring with You—A Functional Fashion Guide

At last, you've been offered a chance to go on a fishing trip. Visions of sunlit afternoons, dappled waters, and huge, flapping fish vying with one another to be on the end of your line flash across your mind. But then, reality intrudes. What should you bring along? Well, open your closet and see what is—and isn't—there.

Just about everyone has a pair of jeans, a cotton shirt, and a heavier shirt—a turtleneck, for instance. Wear these, covered by a jacket or parka for the cool mornings and evenings. As for shoes, sneakers or hiking shoes take care of most situations. Add some sort of hat or scarf for your head (remember, you'll be casting!), some sunglasses (preferably Polaroid), and rain gear, and your basic fishing wardrobe is complete.

Does this sound too easy? Well, you *can* take along a few more items; but keep in mind that too much equipment can be a nuisance. Often, your accommodations will be mighty primitive—no bureaus or hangers, and just a few nails on the walls on which to hang the essentials.

In most cases, each person on the trip lifts her own luggage in and out of cars, boats, and sometimes planes. As far as luggage goes, canvas duffles (preferably waterproof) are the best. And two small bags are better than one large one—not only do they load better but they are also easier to carry. Many fishing camps, you may discover after an already strenuous trek, are on top of a hill . . . a long way up! Duffles today come in all sizes and shapes and are made lighter and stronger and waterproof by the use of various nylon materials.

On any trip, the most valuable outfit of all is a waterproof nylon rain jacket and pants. This material is lightweight and, when folded, takes up very little space. Your outfit should be large enough to fit over several layers of clothing. You can buy it at local sporting goods stores or from the catalogues of Norm Thompson, L. L. Bean, or the Orvis Company, to name only a few sources. Some raingear leaks and some doesn't—and even though it's advisable to test yours *before* starting out on your trip (either by wearing it in the shower or in the rain), you may still get wet. It's a form of Russian roulette.

When it's cold, you can wear your rain pants and rain jacket to cut the wind. And when the weather turns warm, just strip off a few layers and enjoy the sun. The "layered look" is great functional fashion in fishing, too, as well as around town. For early morning cold, wear a cotton shirt as a first layer. Over that, put on a wool shirt or a sweater. Cover this with a down vest or heavy jacket. Add a waterproof windbreaker (or your rain jacket) for the topmost layer. Then, as the temperature rises in the middle of the day, start peeling off a few layers and pack them into the small knapsack you have brought along.

Of all the sports, fishing can call for the most equipment. You have not only various pieces of fishing gear but also your extra clothes (in anticipation of both arctic- and equator-type weather), as well as nonfishing items for reading, photographing, or playing games. Robert Traver, the fishing judge and writer of such books as *Anatomy of a Fisherman*, describes the fishing equipment stored in his garage. It sounds like enough to stock several garage sales.

Whether you are wading or in a boat, take note that you will always be colder in or on the water than you would be on shore. So wear long johns to increase your cold-stamina. Although they are not glamourous they keep out the chills. And gloves, in the early morning or evening, are also a most welcome protection.

Your clothing list will have to adapt to both the type of fishing you will be doing and the type of accommodations you will be staying in. For a backpacking fishing trip, omit as much as possible—every ounce counts. For a floating trip, keep the luggage weight down to twenty-five or thirty pounds. Take along a bathing suit and a long-sleeved cotton shirt for hot, sunny lunch hours, and long pants and a warm jacket for the night. Take sun cream along too.

When staying in a primitive, rustic lodge, you won't need to get dressed up; but bringing a towel, soap, and wire hangers does add to your comfort. Some lodges, on the other hand, are more like resorts; and in such places, extra slacks, a jazzy shirt, and a colorful scarf will see you through the evening hours.

There is no reason why you can't look attractive and feminine while on a fishing trip. Back in 1910, the few adventuresome women who dared to fish wore long skirts for this sport. What a time they must have had making their way through the bushes and over large boulders! But today we are more fortunate (or, simply, wiser). And since women wear pants more often than skirts anyhow, fishing wardrobes are not too different from everyday outfits. Somehow women have managed to look feminine dressed in the same fishing clothes worn by men. Current fashions feature tweedy jackets, caps, felt hats, men's shirts, and boots.

Every woman has her own secret formula to give her a lift at the end of a long day spent wearing bulky waders, an oversized fishing vest, and a camouflaged canvas hat. You can wash your face and hands in a small sliver of your favorite scented English soap. Or you can dab stick perfume behind each ear. By spending an extra few minutes on your bedraggled, tangled hair, you can accomplish miracles. Also, try some hand cream on those sun-dried hands.

In terms of pants, jeans are the most useful ones you can wear on a fishing trip. Whether you are scrambling through thorny berry bushes or climbing over steep, jagged, rocky cliffs, they remain hardy and strong. They show little dirt and keep you comparatively cool in hot weather and act as a good windbreaker when it becomes chilly. If people can ski in blue jeans, they can certainly fish in them. It is best to have two pairs along in case one gets wet. And they do take time to dry.

43

To keep your feet dry, wear waterproofed hiking boots. Sneakers, should it rain suddenly, can prove mighty soggy. But at night you can relax in sneakers, sandals, or soft moccasins. Most hiking boots today are lighter weight than in the past, since they are made of a quick-drying nylon material.

When fishing in a stream, wear either waders or felt-soled shoes. Neoprene waders are probably safest because they float. Make sure your waders are long enough or you'll have trouble going over fences and getting into boats.

For early morning and chilly evenings, a warm parka is a must. A down parka can be rolled up and stuffed into a tiny bag, for easy packing. In milder weather, a thin nylon parka will take care of your needs. Top this off with a wide-brimmed hat (such as a cowboy hat) or a colorful cotton bandana to protect your head from sun, wind, or dust.

If it's very warm, try fishing in cut-offs or shorts. Since fishing clothes are almost exclusively designed for men, there is no reason why you can't make up your own rules of dress (within practical limits, of course), suiting your clothes to your own style, and taste. Happily, stores are beginning to carry fishing clothes in women's sizes. But don't let your desire to be fashionable outweigh your desire to fish. Overly bright colors might spook the fish, so stay away from them.

One of the apparel industry's greatest inventions is the fishing vest. It— as well as many-pocketed safari shirts—*must* have been designed with women in mind! This sleeveless wonder is the angling female's substitute for a bulging purse. Its many pockets—on each side, in back, and even inside— hold everything you'll need on a fishing stream . . . and for the rest of the day, as well. Organize your stash carefully, and you won't waste precious minutes going from pocket to pocket looking for the fly dope or the small fly box that houses the killer fly. The fishing vest has pockets for your sunglasses, your reading glasses, your leaders, your lipstick, your Kleenex, your candy bar, and such other small items.

Waders have advanced the most in recent years. They come in boot length, waist length, and chest length. They are made in thin, durable, easy-to-pack materials for hot weather and thick, warm, snag-proof materials called neoprene. Not only are neoprenes comfy to wear, they are also attractive to all figures—a big plus for women in fishing clothes. Worn with neoprene waders are wading shoes, gravel guards, or boot socks.

In choosing a well-balanced fishing outfit of rod, reel, and line you shouldn't have to pay a great deal. Due to the growing popularity of fishing as well as to the increase in leisure time, there is a large selection of rods.

Beginners should start with a fiberglass rod. They're light and less likely to break or be affected by extreme weather conditions than other rods. Also, they're less expensive. A recommended length is eight and a half feet. Then, once you're more experienced, graduate to a bamboo or graphite rod. Bamboo rods, fishing author Richard Talleur feels, possess a "sweetness of feel." Evie is so enamored of bamboo that, at her insistent instigation, Wally finally, legally bequeathed to her his prize Leonard rod, which he'd received on his twenty-first birthday. But since the appearance of the flexible, lightweight graphite rods, she has now deserted the Leonard bamboo rod for these more versatile rods. But the bamboo rods are still being used on the streams and still very much in demand.

A graphite rod, on the other hand, lets you fish for endless hours without tiring or contracting a tennis elbow, because it is so light. Before you buy your rod, try out a friend's. Charles Ritz, author of *A Fly-Fisher's Life*, says "A faultless rod is one of the best trump cards a fisherman has for attaining his goal." Mel Krieger recommends the new four-piece rods, which are even more compact for traveling.

In buying rods, reels, and lines, get an experienced angler's or sports dealer's advice and assistance. This will ensure that you end up with a balanced outfit. Your expert, keeping in mind what sort of fish you want to catch, will help you decide whether to buy a floating or a sinking line. Dame Juliana Berners had fewer decisions to make—she just spliced horsehairs together to make her lines. But the next historic advance, silk lines, had to be greased daily. These days, synthetic lines are available. They are much improved over previous lines, they last longer, and the price is reasonable.

Binoculars are a handy addition on fishing trips. They allow you to look at unusual birds, families of deer, bear, and small water animals.

A waterproof watch is also a good idea—in fact, we strongly recommend it. Between the rain, wading mishaps, or white-water sprayings in a boat, your watch can become an endangered species.

A small piece of candle is advantageous as a backup for your flashlight and, on a rainy day, to help light a fire. Wooden kitchen matches, stored in two tightly twisted plastic sandwich bags, are indispensable.

Bags and more bags—bags are a fisherman's friend. Use plastic bags to pack your underwear, socks, shirts, etc. They'll keep your clothes both organized and dry. If you're fishing from a boat or hiking you'll appreciate a small canvas bag in which to store your camera, sun and bug lotion, sunglasses, rain gear, and such extras as bird and wildflower identification books, binoculars, chewing gum, comb, lipstick, and bandana. If you'll be on horseback, a rucksack that has shoulder straps is a convenient way to carry your essentials.

Include an emergency supply of candy bars, beef jerky, and even small pieces of cheese in your small canvas bag. A thermos of hot consommé has warmed, cheered, and saved us on many a cold, rainy river trip.

Two other comforts on a fishing trip are the individual packets of Kleenex (store them in your back pocket) and a small, multi-purpose pocket knife.

A three-day women's fishing symposium was given at the Yellowstone conference of the Federation of Fly Fishers, and here's a worthwhile suggestion from that symposium: when you're on the river and the hot sun makes your lips feel too dry, apply some of the Mucelin you use for dry flies. It's lanolin-based and safe.

The Appendix contains a variety of lists that should be useful to you, and will make your trips more enjoyable. Keep in mind that different types of vacations demand individual lists, and use our lists as guidelines only. But if you get a chance to go on a fishing trip, by all means jump at it. It's an adventure in a class of its own.

Minding Your Manners

8

Every sport has its rules, guidelines, and codes of etiquette. In tennis it's court manners to not serve until your opponent is ready, and to not stall unnecessarily between points. In golf there is a certain order in which you tee off. Whether it be pool, basketball, handball, or whatever, all sports have their own protocol.

And, of course, this includes fishing. As early as Dame Juliana Berner's day, fishermen were told how to conduct themselves. She warned anglers to take care of their neighbor's property: "I charge you that you break no man's hedge in going about sports, nor open any man's gates without shutting them again."

One nicety of fishing etiquette is not to enter the water within one hundred feet of another fisherman. The first person in the water has priority. If someone is sitting on the bank to let the water rest, be polite and ask the "resting fisherman" whether or not he or she has finished fishing that particular pool. When you're walking along the stream, stay a good distance away from the edge so that you don't scare the fish. Trout have excellent vision and are more wary than most fish. In clear water they can even spot the waving of your rod on a false cast. As you wade, try not to send mud down the stream. Be considerate and try not to be noisy. Elementary as this may sound, good fishing manners suggest you do not take all the good fishing holes when you're fishing with other people. Alternate the pools to give everyone an equal chance. When the stream is crowded, allow enough space among fellow fishermen to make it rewarding for all.

When two fish together, the first thing to do is discuss the water ahead. Then take turns having first choice of the holes. Some people fish more rapidly than others; some anglers prefer slow pools, while others enjoy fishing in faster water. It's good to be within earshot of each other, and safer too. But you can be too close together, too.

Gertrude and Bob were fishing together in New Zealand on the Eglington River. They'd come a long way for this special fishing and were enjoying the beautiful countryside, friendly people, and, most important, big fish. But soon Gertrude asked Bob not to fish so close to her. After all, she pointed out, they had the whole river to themselves; there was no need for him to crowd her. Right in the middle of their discussion, Gertrude had a strike! All talking stopped. A large trout was running downstream with her line. She tried to stop the fish by putting her thumb on the reel; gradually, she had it under control and began to reel it in.

At this point, Bob realized that he was in the way, and he began reeling in, as well. In lifting his line, he discovered that he was attached to—Gertrude's line! Suddenly there were two lines and one flying fish in the air. But not for long! The airborne fish gave a few flops, and in seconds it was free and swimming happily away. Gertrude was furious and scolded Bob for quite some time—it had been an enormous fish.

The marital relationship may even justify a breach of fishing etiquette, as it did when Gwen and Joe were fishing in Alaska. Late in the day's fishing, Gwen began to cast into the water that Joe was already working (though not particularly successfully). He quickly took offense at her intrusion.

"But Joe, I thought I would fish this lovely spot because today's my birthday."

Neither of them had mentioned this special occasion before, and red-faced Joe's objections suddenly turned to apologies.

When two people are fishing from a boat and only one can cast at a time, it is courteous to cast for equal amounts of time. Rhoda and Dick solved this problem on the McKenzie River by using a pocket parking meter timer: each fished for fifteen minutes before shifting.

One of the curiosities of the fishing circle is how the most esteemed, well-respected citizens will do every honorable thing imaginable—except report *correctly* which fly caught the big one and exactly where on the river the catch was made. Most fishermen follow this practice.

Maybe that is why Robert Traver, describing how fellow fishermen hide their favorite fishing holes, recommends, "Only take dogs, small children and tested fishing pals to your favorite trout spots. Revised moral: on second thought, better only take dogs and small children."

A final suggestion for the neophyte: when returning from a day's fishing, ask your fellow anglers how they did before you blurt out your own successes or failures. But this fishing courtesy may be the hardest of all to follow.

Backpacking
Anglers

9

Their bodies seemed almost weightless as they eased the heavy packs from their shoulders—packs that had felt comfortably light that morning before they started up the steep trail. Sighing with tired satisfaction, they dipped their drinking cups into a tiny cold stream that was rushing headlong into the Sierra lake, set like a small blue jewel in a ring of white granite.

Darkness comes suddenly in the mountains, the two companions knew; so the fire must be laid and their camp made while it was still daylight. They found a neat circle of blackened stones and an old grill, left by a thoughtful camper, perfectly positioned in the curve of a huge rock—the ideal wilderness fireplace. One camper went in search of wood while the other unstrap-

ped sleeping bags, shorty pads, and tarps from the backpacks. Wood was easy to find that evening; they wouldn't need to use the primus stove for cooking. Beneath the shelter of an old lodgepole pine they laid the two sleeping bags side by side, on top of a waterproof tarp. Knowing that Sierra weather is capricious, they looked up at the thin cloudcover and decided to set up their small two-man tent just in case. After the fire was carefully laid, they opened a package of dehydrated stew and emptied it into a lightweight pan to soak so the vegetables would be plump and tender well before dinner time. They blended chocolate pudding mix, which had been divided equally into two paper bowls, with cold water from the stream so it would be creamy and smooth while it was still light.

Now that they had completed all the necessary tasks to keep them comfortable through the cold Sierra night, the two friends sat side by side on a log and unlaced their heavy-soled hiking boots. How good it felt to free their aching feet, slip them into clean white socks, and put on lightweight tennis shoes.

The sun was rapidly approaching the mountain peaks in the west, highlighting their frosty tips with a warm blush. The two friends took off their walking shorts and pulled on long woolen pants. Grabbing down jackets from their packs they began setting up their little four-piece fly rods—there was still time for some fishing before dark. In the Sierra at dusk, there is often a mysterious rise of fish in darkening lakes and streams. Quickly, the friends assembled their rods and attached small reels. And as they ran to the lake, circled with the telltale signs of rising fish, each person selected a fly to tie onto the leader. One chose a tiny dry fly, an Adams; the other selected a little sinking Black Gnat. Because they knew the rise would not last long, they chose separate spots and cast their flies carefully. Almost at once, one of the fishermen hooked a little male brook trout, wearing his spawning colors, just at the mouth of the stream. He fought so valiantly that the campers decided to free him so he could return to his romantic business.

Luck was with the fishermen that evening, and they caught four nice ten-inch trout to supplement that evening's stew. And then, as suddenly as the rise had started, it stopped. The lake was calm—the whole evening was calm—and the sun went down quietly. The campers cleaned the fish and lit the fire, which crackled immediately and comfortably. From the fresh creek, they brought two small buckets of water, placing one of them over the fire. Hot water, the backpacker's crowning luxury, cooks food, makes tea, washes dishes and faces, and warms spirits. The campers sprinkled the fish with salt, pepper, and a few herbs, anointed them with a few precious drops of olive oil and a squeeze of juice from a lemon (whose weight they had considered carefully before putting it into the pack), and wrapped them in aluminum foil.

While dinner was cooking, the two friends spoke in whispers so that they wouldn't disturb the hush of the wilderness night. Looking out, they saw another small campfire, flickering brightly on the lake's opposite shore. But the companions did not find this an intrusion; instead, they were comforted, knowing that other humans were also experiencing this perfect night. Stars studded the night with familiar constellations, and the milky way washed the huge granite mountains. Close at hand, the freshly caught trout sizzled in their foil wrappings, the dehydrated stew changed into a gravy-covered beef-and-vegetable delicacy, and the bowls of now-firm pudding waited to be enjoyed, along with a mug of tea.

With quiet camaraderie, the two friends washed the few dishes, then secured their camp for the night. As the last part of their nighttime ritual, they poured a bucket of water on the embers of the fire. Then they slipped into their sleeping bags and the deep sleep of the outdoors.

Does this sound like a nice way to spend a weekend?

Can you put yourself into this picture?

The two companions in this story could be any two friends who both love the wilderness: a college boy and girl, two men, two women, a husband and wife, a father and son, a mother and son, a father and daughter, or a mother and daughter.

Suggestions for Backpacking Angling Women

For the woman who wishes to immerse herself in a wilderness environment, there is no finer sport than backpacking, and a fly rod fits just as naturally into a backpacking trip as a trout fits into a mountain stream. If you want to experience the solace that comes from shedding the pressures of your daily life, head for the hills—with a carefully planned pack on your back. Go with a companion or with a small group of friends (it's too self-defeating to go with a large group of people). But don't go alone—it's too risky.

When you enter the world of birds and small animals, move quietly—or they will hide and you will never get to see them.

Colin Fletcher, author of *The Complete Walker,* refers to his pack as his "house" on his back, and goes so far as to divide each pack section into "rooms." His pots and pans, stove, plates, and food are his kitchen. His sleeping bag, tent, and ground cover are his bedroom. His shoes, socks, jackets, underwear, and pants are his clothes closet. First he weighs and packs all his necessities carefully. Then he fills the extra spaces with those things that will make his trip more than just a survival exercise. A photographer will certainly want to bring a camera; a botanist will need a plant-identification book; a bird watcher will need a pair of binoculars; and an angler will, of course, need a fly rod and a small box of flies.

Anyone who does any hiking knows that the most important item on a walking trip is a perfect pair of walking shoes. If you are planning to be a backpacking fisherman, invest in a pair of ankle-high, leather-lined boots. After all, your own feet—not a boat or an automobile—will be taking you to the home of the beautiful high Sierra golden trout.

A fly rod weighs somewhere between two and five ounces, a reel and line weighs between four and six ounces, and a little box of assorted dry and wet flies weighs less than a package of chewing gum. An old pair of tennis shoes, with felt or outdoor carpeting glued to the soles, weighs less than a pound and makes adequate wading shoes.

Because this is primarily a fishing book, no attempt will be made to cover all the details of backpacking. Many excellent books written especially for the backpacker are readily available. A trip to your local sporting goods store or mountaineering shop will not only give you access to such books but also the chance to see and buy some of the lightweight cooking utensils, stoves, sleeping bags, tents, walking boots, down jackets, and dehydrated foods that are on the market today. Many stores rent pack frames, tents, and sleeping bags. Renting equipment is an excellent way to try out different products until you find just the right pack or the perfect sleeping bag for you. These stores also carry maps, compasses, pedometers, nature guides, and camp cookbooks. Ron Cordes has written an excellent guide manual, which weighs only three ounces. So strongly does he believe that fly fishing and backpacking are correlated sports that he gave his book two titles: *Fly Fishing for Backpackers* and *Backpacking for Fly Fishermen.*

You don't need to purchase a special rod for your backpacking trips, although it is convenient to have a rod that separates into four sections so that it can fit into a compact case. If you use a conventional, two-sectioned rod, you can tie it to the frame of your pack or carry it in your hand. And a rod in an aluminum rod case can be used as a walking staff, as well.

For a successful hiking and fishing trip, careful planning is essential. For example, when you are packing for a three-day trip into the wilderness be sure to place your last meal in the bottom of your pack and your first meal on top. Label all meals with clearly visible tags. Tie your drinking cup to your belt, and keep your insect repellent, Kleenex, and sunburn cream in a handy, easy-to-reach pocket.

Fishing in high mountain lakes and streams can be difficult. The streams

are usually small and the fish wary. The best way to deal with these suspicious characters is to be cautious when you approach the water, so that
they can't see you. Try a small dry fly, such as a Blue-Upright or an Adams.
Although you will catch most of your fish on a dry fly, be sure to bring some
lightly weighted nymphs in addition. Backpackers have often been known to
look down into the clear, deep water of mountain lakes and see, lying in the
shade of huge rocks, big trout—exasperatingly indifferent to a dry fly but
frequently more responsive to a carefully presented, little, weighted nymph.
Drop it quietly in front of their noses; and get ready for action.

Be sure to take a few sheets of aluminum foil with you. A marvelous
way to cook trout outdoors is to wrap a whole cleaned fish in foil along with
some salt, pepper, herbs, lemon, and a few drops of olive oil. Cook it over
your campfire for a few minutes, then open the foil and taste the perfect
reward of your fishing efforts.

Who's Who in the World of Fish

10

C uriosity and persuasiveness (both supposedly feminine traits) are helpful assets in becoming an angler. A fish usually remains unseen and
well secluded in his own watery dimension, and subtle persuasion is required
to entice him from his river home. The fish is part of the wilderness aes-
thetic, along with wildflowers, wild birds, and wild animals. He is wary of
accepting dinner invitations, fearing that his deliciousness might cast him in
the role of hors d'oeuvre or entrée instead of honored guest.

Once a woman has felt the mysterious tug of communication with an
unseen fish at the end of her line, she will be curious to know everything
about this elusive creature. It is at this point that she will become a fisherman; she will become a protector of wild rivers. She will invite her freshly
caught rainbow trout to dinner and cast him in the role of honored guest as
well as in the role of entrée.

Many types of fish have captured the hearts and imaginations of American anglers, for a fish hooks a fisherman just as securely as a fisherman
hooks a fish. Some men would rather be photographed with their fish than
with their wives; even women anglers have pictures of salmon and trout
adorning their bedroom walls.

Before the United States was sliced into a network of highways and
railways, its relatively inaccessible wild rivers and lakes abounded with thriving, native fish that reproduced plentifully, unharmed by human beings.

Early New England settlers were pleased to find the same leaping Atlantic salmon that they had fished for in the rivers of England, Ireland, and
Scotland. It isn't very well known, but salmon, as well as wild turkey, was
served at the first Thanksgiving feast.

In Adirondack and Catskill streams swam some dashing red-and-yellow
spotted fish with white-edged fins—eastern brook trout—who, popping
their heads out of the water, were surprised to see Pilgrims as well as Indians. The homesick English anglers were entranced with the American
brookie and soon transferred their allegiance from the European brown
trout. Brook trout are still the most beloved fish of New England and New

York fishermen.

Spanish Californios and Northwest mountain men found a completely different breed of salmon coming into western rivers from the Pacific Ocean. It was not the *Salmo salar* found by the East Coast settlers, but *Oncorynchus,* the same genus of salmon found in Japan and China.

Gold miners, soldiers, and covered-wagon families found a green-and-white spotted trout streaked with lines of rosy pink in California, Oregon, and Washington streams. This lovely fish was named, aptly, "rainbow trout."

Lewis and Clark found still another trout in the headwaters of the Missouri River, as did other explorers wandering through Colorado, Montana, Wyoming, and Idaho. They called it a cut-throat trout because a red line like a crimson necklace edged its gill casings.

High in the California Sierra, in the Kern River, lived a beautiful trout colored with the golden iridescence of a tropical fish—the golden trout, loved and respected by early California cattlemen. Brian Curtis, in *The Life Story of the Fish,* tells of two cowboys who scooped a dozen golden trout out of a small stream and carried them in a coffeepot to another larger river, thinking that they would have a better chance to survive. They were right— those transplanted fish flourished in their new home, and filled their new stream with generations of healthy offspring.

In the St. Lawrence and Mississippi River basins, and in the waters of the southern Atlantic states, frontiersmen found the black bass. This Mark Twain sort of fish was the favorite of middle western and southern gentlemen. Brian Curtis says, "The black bass is a typically American fish belonging to a family native only to North America. His character embodies traits which we like to think of as typically American: adaptability, gameness, individuality."

For many decades, each variety of fish remained a citizen of its own home waters, and it wasn't until the advent of the railroad that American freshwater game fish were forced to become peripatetic travelers. Enthusiastic gentlemen, treating the new railroads like a big toy, began to transport the eggs and progeny of their favorite varieties of fish from one river to another. Thus, new species were introduced to lakes and streams that already were populated by other fish called "natives."

For the most part the transplants were successful, and the new citizens prospered. But sometimes, overaggressive newcomers bullied the old natives and usurped their territories. Guided more by naive enthusiasm than reason, many men made transplants that had an absolutely devastating effect on the entire fish populations of that area. Big cannibal fish, put into streams with smaller, gentler species, ate all their hosts' eggs and progeny. Or too many fish were put in an area with a limited food supply, thereby starving all the citizens. In *Where the Bright Waters Meet,* H. Plunkett Greene tells a heartbreaking story of a lovely chalk stream in England that was overplanted with a different strain of brown trout. The entire original fish population starved to death, and the newcomers, lacking sufficient food, were in poor condition.

Fortunately, there are many happy stories connected with these forced fish-migrations. With the almost simultaneous development of the government fish hatchery and the transcontinental railroad, it was only to be expected that fish and fish eggs would make the journey from one coast to another. The striped bass, a native of our Atlantic Coast from the St. Lawrence River to Florida, was one of the first to make the trip. In 1879, less than 150 young stripers journeyed by train from the Navesink River in New Jersey to San Francisco Bay. Another small planting was made a few years later. Today, the descendants of those hardy travelers are flourishing in the Sacramento River and in bays and estuaries up and down the Pacific Coast.

Brian Curtis tells an amusing anecdote about a William Shriver, who could not get over the fact that a careless god had done everything imaginable to make the Potomac a paradise for black bass and had then neglected to put any of the species in that body of water. When the Baltimore and Ohio Railroad was completed across the Alleghenies, the event had one significance to Mr. Shriver: man had provided the link which nature had omitted. He procured a large bucket, punched it full of holes, filled it with bass, and then hung it in the water tank of the locomotive while the train puffed down to the shores of the Potomac. There he released his fish and there have been black bass in the Potomac ever since.

Western species also made triumphant and successful voyages to eastern parts of the United States. The coho salmon, Pacific salmon, and Pacific steelhead adjusted happily to their new homes in the Great Lakes, roaming from lake to stream, emulating the instinctive migratory habits of their ancestors.

In this vast, man-made transmigration of Northern Hemisphere game fish, eastern brook trout went West, western rainbows and cut-throats went East, and the European brown trout came across the Atlantic from England by ship. Trout were transplanted into the southern hemisphere, to such places as South America and New Zealand.

As a result of these transplants, the present-day California and Oregon angler will find brookies, rainbows, cut-throats, and browns all swimming in the same stream. And the Massachusetts and Vermont fisherman shouldn't be surprised to see rainbows and browns swimming right along with the eastern brook trout. Surprisingly, it is the delicate eastern brook trout that has made the most dramatic adaptation to the severe granite environment of the California high Sierra. This trout can withstand the ice and low temperatures of Sierra lakes and streams even better than the rainbow trout, a California native. Anyone who has fished in Montana and Wyoming knows that the big European brown trout is now a healthy, fighting citizen of the Beaverhead and the Green Rivers. The rainbow is the dearest and most adaptable of all of these beauties, thriving in any cool stream or lake where there is enough food and oxygen. It is the perfect guest, the perfect host, the perfect fish.

Each breed of game fish has its own distinctive character and personality. Some have natural migratory habits of heroic proportions. All salmon (both Pacific and Atlantic) and some trout are anadromous fish, born with a round-trip ticket in their pockets. Hatched from eggs in freshwater streams, they seem to have a touch of salt in their souls; while still young they swim and drift with the currents from their home waters, through lakes and down rivers, until they reach the ocean. Once in the heavier salt water, their systems undergo a metabolic change that enables them to adjust to the new environment. Living most of their lives in the ocean, anadromous fish feed on plankton and other small sea animals. They grow to huge proportions, blown-up versions of their freshwater selves. Then, mysteriously—sometimes after a period of many years—these large saltwater creatures yearn to return to the small brook where they were hatched. Spurred by mating instincts, both male and female begin the long journey back to their home waters. They travel not by train, ship, or plane, but by the gigantic force and energy of their own muscular drive. Once they re-enter fresh water they stop feeding, relying instead on the strength and vitality that they accumulated while living in the ocean. They desperately need to get upstream, through the current, over waterfalls, across huge lakes, and back to the spawning grounds where they themselves were born.

Scientists and poets have puzzled over this uncanny ability of salmon and sea-going trout to find their way back to the identical location where they emerged from the egg sac. Obviously, this homing instinct resembles the precise, inner clockwork of migratory birds; but scientists' latest theory is that fish have a keen sense of smell and can remember the scents of their home waters.

With the exception of a few strains of landlocked salmon (Ouananiche and Sebago are Atlantic salmon that are confined to lakes), all salmon are anadromous. Pacific salmon—chinook, silver, sockeye, chum, and pink—

make the return trip only once. After the female lays her eggs and the male fertilizes them, both parents die. The dying sockeye salmon is the often-photographed "last supper" for the Alaskan brown bear before it goes into hibernation. The Pacific salmon, primarily a commercial fish or a saltwater sport fish, does not take readily to a fly on its homeward journey; but the fly fisherman loves and admires its noble characteristics nevertheless, and often encounters this fish performing its marriage rites in small western streams. The late Roderick Haig-Brown wrote a biography of a chinook salmon called *Return to the River,* a moving and informative account of this mysterious and admirable fish.

The Atlantic salmon, the salmon of Labrador, Greenland, Maine, and Quebec, used to be abundant in East Coast rivers as far south as New York but was driven away by industrial pollution and is the same *Salmo salar* that is native to Scotland, England, Ireland, France, Germany, Sweden, and Norway. Several times during its life, it may make its long, upstream journey to spawn. Some anglers feel that the leaping Atlantic salmon is the most dramatic game fish of all. It is a muscular mixture of John Barrymore, Rudolph Nureyev, Houdini, and Samson: actor, ballet dancer, escape artist, and strongman. Juliana Berners, encountering the Atlantic salmon in fifteenth-century England, said, "The salmon is a noble fish, but cumbersome to catch being only found in deep places of great rivers."

The steelhead, actually a cousin of the Atlantic salmon and possessing many of its fine characteristics, is *Salmos gairdneri*—the same genus and species as the rainbow trout. Steelhead are ocean-going rainbows, sea trout. Born in freshwater streams, as they mature they move out into the Pacific Ocean. There, they follow much the same pattern as the Atlantic salmon: eating and growing into bigger and stronger versions of rainbow trout, and returning to their home waters to spawn. Superb game fish, they take a fly with enthusiasm and make such rivers as California's Klamath, Oregon's Rogue, and British Columbia's Sustut famous "steelhead streams."

A cut-throat trout may also be anadromous. These seagoing cut-throat are sometimes called harvest trout because they return to spawn in the autumn. In the British Isles, ocean-migrating brown trout are known by many different names: sea trout, salters, white trout peal, sewing, or Candlemas trout.

As the human population in the United States increased, the fish population declined. Dams were built on many of the wild rivers, and these cut off the fish's access to upstream spawning grounds. Industrial wastes and other pollutants depleted the oxygen supply to such an extent in some lakes and rivers that they could no longer support life. The big Great Lakes lake trout were almost completely destroyed by pollution, siltation, and an infestation of lamprey eels. The new highway system made all but the remotest areas accessible.

The Department of Fish and Game (part of the Department of the Interior) and the state fisheries realized that measures had to be taken to replenish the declining supply of game fish. Thus they established hatcheries close to most major streams. When fish raised in these nurseries became big enough to fend for themselves, they were planted in the rivers. But many of these hatchery-bred fish, living in the river for just one season, were unable to reproduce in their new environment. These one-season fish are known as "catchables," because they are put in the river for fishermen to catch, much the same principle as planting a field of daisies and then inviting everyone who enjoys daisy picking to come for the harvest. A wild fish that is indigenous to a body of water is known as a "native," and a transplanted variety of fish that becomes firmly established, reproducing and thriving along with "natives," is called a "wild" fish.

In recent years, people have become more and more aware that the earth's resources are not limitless. Private citizens, as well as biologists and government officials, have taken a new interest in the plight of the fish. Whales, seals, and dolphins (which are mammals, not fish) are the particular darlings of many conservationists. But many endangered fish species have begun to swim along with whale and dolphin into the concerned hearts of many people. Happily for the waning population of the Atlantic salmon, groups such as the Atlantic Salmon Association, Restoration of the Atlantic Salmon in America (RASA), and L'Association Pour Le Sumon de L'Atlantique are fighting for its preservation on both sides of the Atlantic.

This splendid fish has been in trouble for a long time. Once so abundant in New York rivers that masters were prohibited by law from serving their servants salmon more than once a day, the Atlantic salmon was quickly driven out of the state. Robert Barnwell Roosevelt's *Game Fishes of the North*, published in 1862, says, "Hendrick Hudson, on ascending the river he discovered, was particularly struck with their immense numbers, and continually mentions 'great stores of salmon.' The last unhappy fish that was seen in the Hudson had his adventurous career terminated by the net, near Troy, in the year 1840."

Driven out of New England by dams and industry, the original East Coast Atlantic salmon runs are now found only in Canadian streams. Recently, this fish has been plagued by deep-sea commercial trawlers that, with their supersonic instruments, have found its ocean feeding grounds.

Rachel Carson, one of the greatest champions the American fish ever had, describes another appalling tragedy experienced by the Atlantic salmon in her book, *Silent Spring*. A chapter called "Rivers of Death" gives an account of how a careless spraying of DDT to control the spruce budworm in 1954 killed all the insects and fish on the Miramichi River in New Brunswick. Miraculously, a few salmon did escape the holocaust, and gradually the Miramichi is building a new salmon population.

As human beings begin to realize that the protection of our natural resources is a worldwide problem, there is more than a ray of hope for many fine fish species. On both a local and an international level, people are taking intelligent steps to shield these species from further destruction, through such actions as limited fish kill, catch and release, and barbless hooks.

If you are an amateur botanist or ornithologist, you already know how important it is to have a good wildflower or wild bird identification book. So if you intend to become a fisherman buy a good freshwater game fish book, complete with color plates and lists of family characteristics.

Each fisherman tends to develop an emotional affinity with particular breeds of fish. This involvement sometimes becomes part of the fisherman's own personality, so that people may say:

"He is a brown-trout-loving school teacher."

"That lumberman is a silver-salmon fisherman."

"That terrific secretary is nuts about striped bass."

"That woman kisses her rainbows before she puts them back."

You don't have to be a baseball fan to know where "Catfish" Hunter got his name. Catfish, in various forms, are found all over the United States. Their whiskery faces, lovingly associated with "down home" fishing, feed on the bottom of warm lakes and ponds.

Many people love the bass. They associate it with good times. Many of these bass belong to different families. The striped bass is a sea bass, a saltwater fish that moves into fresh water to spawn. The black bass belongs in the same genus with the highly popular panfishes: sunfish, bluegill, and crappies. These are thought of as sunshine fish—warm weather fish—fun fish, less elite than the elusive cold-water trout. Largemouth bass and bluegill are usually stocked in farm ponds and serve as predators to keep down populations of smaller fish.

Get yourself a fishing rod and a few flies (or even a moss-filled container of red worms or night crawlers). Then go out and get acquainted with a fish.

Some of Our Best Friends are Rivers

F rom Roscoe, New York, to Anchorage, Alaska, anglers go through the identical ritual of preparing themselves for a day on the river. They not only dress alike, in battered "old-shoe" clothes, but, as they dig nervously through their fly boxes, selecting flies of outlandish color combinations and diverse sizes, they even talk alike in fishing clichés. Then they load their fishing vests with enough equipment to supply all the fishermen from coast to coast.

Similarly, their happy-hour discussions could easily come off a tape recorded in any bar where the bourbon, scotch, or vodka fills the glasses. First

comes the graphic description of the "big one" that broke away. Then, invariably, the conversation turns to each fisherman's favorite trout stream. Soon the conversation becomes a heated debate: which *are* the most famous fishing rivers? Everyone has his/her own pets, and no one agrees with anyone else.

If you want to be part of this one-upsmanship game, make yourself familiar with these names and their locations: Easterners brag about the Battenkill in Vermont, as well as about the Esopus Creek in the Catskills in New York. Women from the Woman Flyfisher's Club boast about the Neversink River in upper New York. There are those who feel the Letort Spring Creek in Pennsylvania offers the most classic trout fishing. Farther west, fishermen praise the Ausable in Michigan. And while you're remembering names, take note of the Green River in southwestern Wyoming and the Madison in Yellowstone and Montana. Other people recommend fishing the Firehole of Yellowstone Park and The Henry's Fork of the Snake River in Idaho.

Evie recommends Silver Creek, near Sun Valley in Idaho. One of her most exciting fishing experiences took place at this famous chalk stream in a lovely meadow. Her guide, Paul Ramlow, a former head of the Sun Valley Ski School, was an expert fisherman. Wading in this corkscrew stream, they could not only feel fish brushing against their waders but, even more exasperating, they could see them resting in their "holding pattern," just waiting to be tempted. Paul and Evie spotted an enormous rainbow and she began casting for it. The fly landed a few feet in the front of the trout, gently floated over its nose—and the fish ignored the fly! After a few more casts, Evie reeled the fly in and changed it. But again, the trout rejected the fly. This time, Evie not only changed the fly but switched to a smaller one. This process was repeated four more times; tension was mounting. Finally, Evie used a fifth fly—a size 18 on a 5X leader—and the trout rolled up and snatched it. Evie was exuberant—but a bit prematurely. She played the fish for ten minutes. Then, suddenly, it got free and swam away. Such a small fly could hardly be expected to hold so large a fish, but there was always the outside chance. However the "campaign" and "battle" (while they lasted) made this an unforgettable fishing experience, despite the fact that Evie never got to photograph—or even weigh—her fish.

Westerners will speak up loud and clear for Hat Creek in northern California, for the Pit River, a tributary of the Sacramento, and for the Rising River. The Deschutes and McKenzie in Oregon are among the loveliest of rivers. The Yellowstone and Big Hole, both in Montana, are favorites of many, as is Talarik Creek in Alaska.

But after all this effusive, justified praise, these talkative fishermen are apt to put on a long face and bemoan how fishing has gone downhill and how these rivers just aren't what they used to be.

If your group isn't weighing the merits of favorite trout streams, maybe it's because its members are discussing pet wild rivers, where they've caught large salmon and steelhead and trout.

Such rivers as the Rogue in southwestern Oregon or the Middle Fork of the Salmon River in Idaho are becoming more popular every year. A trip down the Rogue is highly recommended and can be enjoyed in one of four ways. For the hardy, there's a backpacking hike from Graves Creek to Illahe. It is a beautiful, well-marked trail, with excellent camping sites enroute. Allow four or five days to relax, fish, and absorb the beauty of the wilderness area. Another option is to come by boat, with guides, and camp out. It is rewarding to be so close to the river and to live on such primitive land. The last option is to stay in lodges along the way. These are very comfortable and you'll really enjoy sharing fishing stories at dinner while you eat home-cooked meals at long, family-style tables. Whichever choice you make, you can travel through exciting white-water rapids each day, picnicking at noon and fishing the best waters enroute. A fourth option is to float down on a raft you run yourself. A great many people do this—but you should do it only if the members of your party are experienced at both camping and white-water boating. Recently, permits have been required to camp on the Rogue.

It's the variety of water that makes this river so unusual. Long, smooth, calm stretches contrast with thunderous, roaring, white water. Rainie Falls, with its ten-foot drop, has been called "the widow maker." A few brave souls (foolishly) take their rafts over it, but most boats are lined down the fish ladder—a tight, rocky chute that the salmon use to go up the river to spawn. But fish can maneuver through this chute better than humans can; even the experts find guiding their boats through these rapids difficult. A little farther down the river Tyee Rapids at some water levels is tricky and difficult. Wildcat Rapids is another thriller—you must keep left of the island and go through a narrow slot between the island and a submerged boulder. Smooth stretches do alternate between each of these rapids, but they aren't the main attraction. Upper and Lower Black Bar Rapids also give exciting rides. Five miles below Winkle Bar, on the lower river, is Mule Creek Canyon. Its forty- to fifty-foot-high rock walls squeeze the river into a tight, narrow passageway—sometimes it's only fifteen feet wide. Halfway through is the famous Coffee Pot, a scary piece of water that can trap you into a whirlpool and send you round and round. More heavy white water follows in Blossom Bar Rapids. Finally, as you go farther down, the river widens and becomes more civilized. In the lower river, the fishing often is better—the fish run bigger and heavier. And what you lose in scenic beauty, you gain in larger fish.

In the fall, the frost causes the leaves of oak and dogwood trees and the poison oak and vine maple to change colors to brilliant oranges, yellows, and reds. The rain brightens these colors even more—but it's a mixed blessing. There can be a lot of it, and unless you are prepared, it can be mighty cold and pretty uncomfortable. Fall fishing can be tremendous when you catch four- or five-pound steelhead; or it can be slow, with most fish being "half-pounders"—actually weighing from one to one and one-half pounds. But the beauty of this river will make up for a day of disappointing fishing. If you wish to fish longer than four days, try Rutledge's Ranch at Illahe in the lower section of the river. The fish are often bigger and more plentiful. Near Grant's Pass there is Morrison's Lodge for pleasant fishing.

In the spring, the fishing is over—but the white dogwood is at its height, and it is unforgettable. When you float down the river, you become part of a world in which shy deer feed along the banks, playful otter slide down the rocks into the water, and, occasionally, black bear prowl along the river's edge in search of berries and dead fish. Overhead, a four-foot blue heron may flap its large wings as it searches for fish, and down on a log a water ouzel may diligently do its daily pushups. A kingfisher may rattle forth an announcement that your boat is coming. Mergansers, mallards, and pintails may follow your boat, and occasionally you may be fortunate enough to see a bald eagle, an osprey, or a snowy egret.

Fishing on the Rogue varies year by year, depending on weather conditions, the opening of the dam, and the number of fishermen allowed to fish the waters. Some years the fish run big and are plentiful, but in recent times the fishing has been poorer and the fish have run smaller—more and more, the catch is half-pounders. The number of boats and rubber rafts have increased alarmingly. Campsites are being overused, and the crowded river has lost some of its magic. This primitive wilderness river is being turned into a busy water-highway. Untrained people are taking on water for which they are not prepared. Accidents are more frequent. But the "traffic" down the river is now regulated, and hopefully the fishing limit will be reduced, or a rule to release all fish for a few years will be made, so the fish population can build up again.

Also highly recommended is a trip down the Middle Fork of the Salmon River. One group's trip was more exciting than anticipated; in the end it proved quite frightening. It took place at the end of June, when the early warm weather had melted the mountain snows too quickly, swelling the rivers and causing some to overflow. A group of ten old college friends from the University of California had traveled from Boston, Los Angeles, Berkeley, and San Francisco to make this long-planned trip, and they were determined to go, no matter what. Prince Helfrich, a famous Oregon fishing guide, warned that the high waters might be dangerous; secretly, he knew that a boat ahead had overturned and drowned a man on the trip. Subsequently another boat ahead would also overturn, drowning the guide and one of the passengers. Later it was learned that Sir Edmund Hillary, the famous mountaineer, had refused to go on the river after seeing its condition. But the group stubbornly insisted on attempting the trip. It wasn't long before these people found out that not only was the water high and hazardous but also that the rains were coming—and didn't plan to let up. Each day, the river rose higher. The guides found maneuvering the McKenzie-type wooden boats a challenge; they warned their passengers to sit only in the center of the boat and to hold on to the sides at all times. Rapids with such names as Powerhouse, Artillery, and Pistol Creek did not give this increasingly nervous group too much confidence.

Each day the campers dried their sleeping bags and gear in front of the campfire. As they moved on from campsite to campsite, they felt the tension of their boatmen. When the wet and scared group of campers finally arrived at the takeout area, they were happy just to be in one piece, even though the heavy rains had kept them from seeing much scenery or setting up their rods and fishing. But they knew there would be more trips forthcoming, in which they could enjoy the hot springs, visit the Indian caves, look for bighorn sheep grazing on the hillsides, and—of course—fish this famous river.

Alaskan fishing devotees brag about their catches on the Brooks, Copper, and Kulik Rivers. And eastern Canada fishing fans talk about the Restigouche, Matapedia, and Miramichi rivers, which often reward them with a catch of large Atlantic salmon.

Everyone has her own favorites, and that's all to the good. If all fishermen preferred the same water, they would be lined up body-to-body—as on opening day in the New York streams. There is a variety not only of tastes, but also of conditions. Over the years, you learn that there will be good days and not-so-good days. These uncertainties are one of the charms of the sport. And fishing has so many charms that it's hard to disagree with Robert Traver: "Trout fishing is so enjoyable it really should be done in bed."

Questions You've Always Wanted to Ask a Fish

ave you ever wondered what a fish thinks and sees? Do you look as huge as King Kong to a fish? Can it hear you talking or smell you? Do the artificial flies really fool it? How smart is a fish, anyhow? These questions may give you something to think about when you're biding time while the fish aren't biting. The more you understand about fish and how they behave, the better you'll get at catching more fish. Countless scientific volumes have been written in answer to these questions. Here are only a few basic answers.

Has a trout a brain? Yes, but its largest part is the optic section. A trout uses a very small part of its brain for thought; primarily it operates by instinct, reflexes, and conditioned reflexes. This explains why this fish scares so easily.

As you are removing the hook from your fish's jaw, do you worry that your fish is feeling pain? When hooked, a fish apparently experiences more fright than pain, especially when pressure is put on the line. Fish don't feel pain the way humans do.

Have you ever wondered whether a trout sleeps? In a sense it does—it points its head into the stream, stays in motion, and keeps its eyes open (but switches off its senses). In this position, the trout can turn at any moment. Trout sleep mostly at night, while other fish that are bottom feeders stay awake and eat after dark. So when your fish won't react to your fly, it may just be catching up on its sleep.

People have argued for decades about how much a trout sees and whether it can distinguish color. The eyesight of a fish differs from ours because of the position of its eyes on the sides of its head and the angle caused by the refraction of the water. Because of this refraction, fish see things upwards, above the surface, through a circle (as though through a porthole). Fish viewing objects below the surface have single peripheral vision to each side, with a small common field before both eyes.

Many fish are said to have binocular vision. This means seeing an object with both eyes simultaneously. Trout have limited binocular vision because of the placement of their eyes. They see with only one eye at a time, but the image they see with one eye goes directly to the opposite optic brain center. Because of where their eyes are placed, fish see objects directly in front of or somewhat above them best.

Ophthalmologists have made detailed studies of the eyesight of the trout. They have found that the trout is nearsighted and can see clearly for only twenty to thirty feet. Objects beyond that distance appear blurred. A trout sees color better in bright light than in weak light, and its eyes are sensitive to ultraviolet rays. When a hatch is out and there are large numbers of similar insects floating on the water, a trout will feed on the hatch and refuse all objects of other sizes and colors.

Inside a fish's eye there is a wonderful reflector, known as *tapetum lucidum,* in the back of the retina and extending around in front of the iris. It is this reflector that makes it possible for a fish to see in the dark. No wonder the New Zealanders fish with success in the pitch dark. Evie and Wally tried it once on a moonless night on the Waiau River in South Island. They were staying in the small town of Te Anau, and they boated to Bear Island for a light supper before fishing. Darkness came around eight o'clock and, as if a cannon shot signaled the fish to begin feeding, an enormous rise appeared on the water. Fish were feeding all over; they could be heard noisily breaking surface, sucking in their food, and plunging under water. Evie cast toward the sound and hoped for the best. Suddenly she had a tremendous strike and felt the fish give a hard pull and run. The reel began to sing, and soon Evie realized that the fish, line, and line-backing were headed out to another lake, river—or maybe to the sea! But even though the fish broke the line and Evie never saw the fish, still the experience was a thrill. In her imagination that fish will always be a monster . . . and each year it grows a few inches.

What does a fish see when you cast your fly on the water? He sees sparkle on the water, caused by the fly's hackles forming an indentation on the water's surface. This sparkle attracts the trout's attention, and if the fish wishes to eat, it will move under the light pattern in order to see the sparkle with both eyes. A fish is interested mostly in the light pattern and believes it is a natural fly. The color of the fly is of secondary importance. In fact, there is disagreement about whether a fish that is deep in the water can see color in a floating fly. Brian Curtis is one authority who thinks a fish can't. The other school of thought is that a fish that is down deep sees the color of a dry fly, while a fish lying near the surface notes the sparkle rather than the color. A fish sees the underside of a fly, illuminated by the light reflected off the bottom of the stream. A fly on the surface seen from the bottom comes out in entirely different colors. It is agreed that fish strike a submerged wet fly for its color, form, and size since it makes no light pattern and lacks sparkle. Therefore, a dry fly, which sparkles on the surface, has an advantage over a wet fly.

One wonders just what attracted Gwen's salmon on the Eagle River in Labrador. It was her first day's fishing of the pool nicknamed "The Bath Tub." Standing on some large rocks, she fished a small piece of water just above some boiling, turbulent falls. Situated to the right was the base of the falls. The salmon in this pool were resting before making the strenuous, leaping trip up the waterfall to their spawning grounds. Gwen's first cast evoked a spectacular response! Silvery, muscular torpedoes began springing up out of the water. Gwen cast her fly in front of an enormous, rolling fish, which grabbed the "brown bug" and dropped like a heavy stone to the bottom of the pool. Alvin, the guide, said, "It's the big fish. Keep your rod up and stay calm." The salmon was strong, crafty, and determined. It sulked on the bottom, shook its head, and lunged toward the current. All Gwen could do was keep a steady pressure between herself and the fish, giving and taking, like a satisfying conversation.

It was now lunch time and Gwen played the fish for half an hour. Although her arms were so tired that she could hardly hold her rod upright, she was determined to get that fish, and she kept it faced into the current. After fifty-five minutes, she finally was able to reel it, slowly, into Alvin's net. The big salmon was handled gently with wet hands and weighed in at sixteen pounds. Alvin gave it artificial respiration by moving it gently back and forth in the current so that its gills could expand with the oxygen-filled water. The big monster rested by a rock for a few minutes before it swam back into the river. If Gwen hadn't remembered to keep this fish in check, it would have headed for the falls and broken away. In fact, Joe thinks that Gwen landed the big salmon because she played it gently, and didn't fight it hard enough to make it react by struggling out into the current and so downstream. Alvin, more accustomed to male anglers than to Gwen's more feminine technique, had been sure she would lose it. He had even said, "You can't land a salmon here."

But the question remains. Why did the salmon strike? Because of the sparkle on the water? Or did the fly's color attract it? Did it think it was a natural fly? Did the moving object annoy it so much that it struck it in anger? Returning salmon don't feed in fresh water—but this one may have been giving support to the generally accepted (but unproven) theory that the salmon hits the fly because it remembers feeding as a parr (young salmon). We'll never know!

How fish feed is another question. We know that they find their food and feed both on the bottom and on the surface. They station themselves where they can find the most food with the least effort. In clear water you can watch a fish positioning its nose in front of the food, opening its mouth, and sucking in a mouthful of water containing the food. Young fish, like puppies, will eat anything. Many fish have learned to eat unusual food, such as bread, grubs, cheese, and worms. But small fish eat mostly insects or small fish. Trout and steelhead are often selective and will strike only one type of fly. Other times they will be less selective and rise for May Flies, Midges, Stone Flies, etc. When at sea, steelhead eat squid, greenling, and amphipods. When they return to the river they eat like trout. When they travel upstream, since they are going up the river to breed, they eat less. Salmon do not take the lure because they are hungry, but because of a conditioned reflex. They hit it in a fit of madness.

Some fishermen have noticed that fish feed on the surface when the barometer is on the rise. If the barometer is falling or low, the fish feed on the bottom and are more likely to shun a dry fly. Other eating habits show that trout are hungriest in good or subdued light but not darkness or bright sunshine. Salmon want light before they will feed. Sea trout (steelhead) will take food in the dark. Rain will often dislodge food into the river and cause all types of fish to feed.

A fish sees a fisherman standing on shore as being up in the air rather than on the bank of the stream. (Chagall, who painted floating people, must have had eyes on the sides of his head.) That's why it's important to stay down low when you approach the water's edge. A fish can't see a low object, because light rays approaching the water from a low angle reflect from the surface, rather than penetrate it. A trout does not see shapes as humans do. To a trout, an object looks much flatter than it really is. (Somewhat like the distorted mirror in the fun house.) Light rays reflecting from an object and entering the water are bunched up when they reach the trout's eye. People appear Lilliputian in height but very wide in breadth. For example, to a trout a man standing six feet above the water at a distance of fifteen feet appears to be only fifteen inches high. But despite these compressed height measurements, the man's width is still seen realistically. We must all look like professional football players or Humpty-Dumpty characters to a fish. If a trout can see *us* on shore, think how much our *rod* shows! Often our motions, more than our presence, scare the fish.

Not only do fish have binocular vision (seeing an object with both eyes) but they also have monocular vision (seeing separately with each eye). If the sun is blinding a fish on one side, it can still see your shadow with its other eye. Also, trout see better at sundown when the light is subdued. At this time the fisherman is less visible but the fly can still be seen as well as ever. This could explain why fishing is usually best just before darkness.

Therefore, remember to keep your movements to a minimum and to walk slowly and quietly to streamside so that your shadow does not show on the water. Place yourself and your rod as close to the surface as possible and try to stand behind the fish as much as you can. Waders have an advantage over bank fishermen. Wear dull-colored clothing such as green, gray, or tan and avoid bright colors, especially red.

If you are choosing a fly for color, studies show that red and orange are visible near the surface but not in deep water. These colors in particular are said to bring out anger and aggressiveness in fish. Blue, green, violet, and dark colors have high reflectance and can be seen more clearly in deep water. Black has low reflectance, while white has high. Some scientists claim that white, silver, and yellow get the fish's attention best, and that blue is productive if the object is down deep or viewed from far away. Combinations of yellow and black or yellow and dark blue work well. Combining red and green often causes fish to shy away. On bright days, the best non-imitative fly is a light one with plenty of tinsel. On dull days, use dark flies that don't glitter.

Does a fish have a sense of smell and hearing? Its sense of smell is more acute than its ability to hear. A fish smells from its nostrils, in the front of its head. These nostrils connect with a cavity that holds nerve cells and is sensitive to smells. The senses of smell and taste are closely related in a fish. Its tongue has taste buds (as does the human tongue) and can differentiate between sour, salt, and bitter flavors. A fish cannot taste sweetness. Trout are said to be disturbed by human scent, and for this reason some people argue that we shouldn't place our hands in the water or handle our lures more than necessary. Supposedly, insect repellent and gasoline (transferred from your fingers to the fly) turn a fish off. A trout is so sensitive that it can sense the movement through the water of a nearby fly, even when it can't see it. So delicate is the sense of smell in trout and salmon that these fish can find their way back to their native rivers merely by the scent of the water.

A trout has an inner ear embedded in its skull, and noises warn it, frighten it, and cause it to flee. It "hears" through the water not with its ears but with the lateral line—an important nerve that runs beneath the skin where the scales are located—along the sides of its body. This nerve senses minute vibrations in the water. The trout's ear gives it a sense of equilibrium and position. So keep in mind that a noisy approach will result in poor or no fishing. Water is an excellent conductor of sound, and sound travels five times faster in water than in air.

Fishermen gathered around the fire at night often discuss weather and temperature changes and ask whether fish can sense these. Like the storybook princess who could feel a pea twenty mattresses beneath her, a fish can feel even one degree of change. It will only eat in certain temperatures. It can die if the temperature suddenly rises ten degrees (anyone experienced with tropical fish tanks sorrowfully remembers the dead, belly-up fish he/she found after the thermostat had gone awry). In cold weather the fish won't feed when the air is warmer than the water. Trout generally feed when the water is between thirty-five and sixty-five degrees. The best temperature is forty-five to sixty-five degrees.

These days, scientists are literally talking with—and listening to—dolphins and porpoises, and learning a lot about the human species, in the process, as well. If we could communicate directly with fish, too, what a wealth of information and insight we would obtain! For now, though, we'll have to content ourselves with the information we do have—and with the sheer pleasure of sharing the fish's world, as fishermen.

Notes about Knots

13

E ver since the frustrated Alexander whacked away with his sword at the Gordian Knot, people have been intrigued and puzzled by the intricacies of knot tying. Perhaps it is because all of us have, in the center of our beings, a neat little knot tied for us by the doctor who separated us from our mothers.

It isn't only sailors, fishermen, and surgeons who are dependent on well-tied knots. All people who wrap packages, tie up dogs or horses, wear neckties, or put ribbons in their hair need to know this skill too. Knot tying is so intertwined with our culture that we say a tense person is "tied up in knots," an indecisive one is "at loose ends," a hysterical one is "unstrung," and a tired young mother is "at the end of her rope." Even the marriage ceremony "ties the knot."

If you are going to become a fisherman, you will have to learn something about knot tying because, unfortunately, scotch tape and safety pins just will not hold your fishing line together (or affix your fly to the leader). The process of assembling a fishing line is loosely based on the principle behind the old song, "The neck bone's connected to the back bone, the back bone's connected to the hip bone," etc. The reel's connected to the backing, the backing's connected to the fly line, the fly line's connected to the leader, and the leader's connected to the fish hook (or fly). All of these connections are made with specific knots. If you happen to be married to the former knot-tying champion of Butte County you may ask him to assemble your line; but since the chances of this are slim, your best bet is to start studying good diagrams of fishing knots. You will be delighted to find that many of these knots, in spite of their salty seafaring names, are old familiar friends that you have used all your life.

Automatically, you tie your apron strings behind your back with a reef knot ending in a double loop—knowing that one pull of the string will release the apron so that you can answer the doorbell. So that your dog won't follow the kids to school, you secure him to the fence post with a loop and two half hitches. You tie your packages with a packer's knot. You use two bowlines when you make a swing out of an old tire. You braid your little

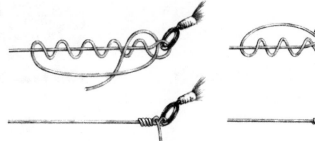

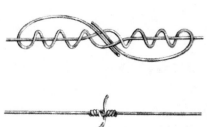

IMPROVED CLINCH KNOT: Strongest knot for tying a fly onto the leader.

BLOOD KNOT: Used to tie two pieces of leader material together.

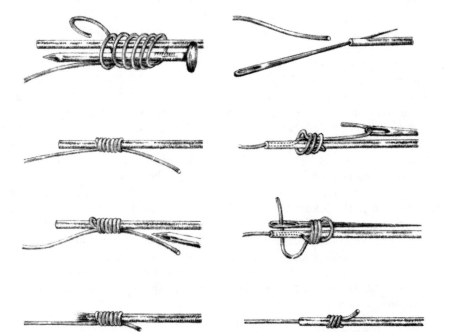

NAIL KNOT: Used to tie leader onto line.

NEEDLE KNOT: This knot may be used either for attaching a leader to a line or for attaching nylon backing.

TURLE KNOT: Not as strong as an Improved Clinch Knot but is sometimes used to tie a fly onto a leader when the eye of a hook is turned down. This keeps the fly from standing on its nose.

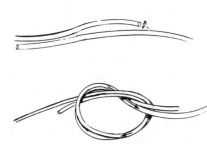

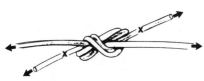

SURGEON'S KNOT

75

daughter's pigtails with the same plaits used by Nantucket whale fishermen (except that you lash the ends with red ribbons rather than twine).

Macramé is an old art that recently has regained popularity. The lovely, intricate, lacy patterns that a macramé artist can form are merely creative combinations of double half-hitches (clove hitches), square knots, and larkshead knots. So you can see that knot tying can also be a very feminine craft.

The old traditional art of knot tying is still newsworthy. In October 1978, the *San Francisco Chronicle* featured the discovery of a new knot on its front page. The inventor of this knot, an English surgeon named Edward Hunter, named his new creation "The Hunter's Bend." Its outstanding quality is its ability to secure nylon cording without slippage.

An enthusiastic fly fishing woman, Gertrude Levison, developed a fine new twist of her own as an easy-to-tie substitute for a barrel knot. It is a good method for joining two strands of filament of differing diameters and is similar to the old surgeon's knot.

The surgeon's knot is often neglected for the barrel knot. Yet it will safely tie lines of different diameters and it can be tied with your eyes closed or when dusk comes all too soon. It is the easiest, quickest, and safest knot . . . take our word!

Clinch knots, barrel knots, nail knots, and loop knots are the main knots that a fly fisherman must master. You can learn them quickly and tie them adeptly with your own hands—and if these hands are accustomed to knitting, crocheting, needlepoint, embroidering, or doing macramé, you'll find knot tying all the easier, because it, too, is a textile art.

The next time you give up smoking, take up knot tying. It keeps the hands busy and doesn't pollute the air.

When the Fish Aren't Biting

14

Y ou try and try—you do everything right—you choose the perfect fly—and still not a bite! But don't despair. There are lots of options. (You might even like some of these ideas more than fishing itself!)

Rock hunting can keep you going for hours. Gather agate and jasper or jade along the gravel bars. Collect some interesting rocks for your next flower arrangement. Specialize in a particular scarce color. Choose a certain shape, such as egg, heart, square, triangle, or rocks with holes in the middle. Look for shapes that are miniature pieces of modern sculpture, or rocks with a combination of colors or designs. Often you can pick up petrified wood that is ash white on the surface and black inside. How about stones to paint on, or to cut and polish? There are endless possibilities, and they make nice souvenirs of your trip. If you want to go all out and graduate to gems, consult Mary L. T. Brown's *Gems for the Taking* or Frederick H. Pough's *Field Guide of Rocks & Minerals*.

Panning for gold in some states is another great pastime, but don't expect to pay for your trip with what you find. Those glittery gold flakes are probably Fool's Gold. But if it's the sport that turns you on, all you need is a flat pan, such as a pie plate or light skillet (although the standard gold pan is the best). Burn the pan over the fire so that its bottom is not greasy. Burn it until it turns blue. From around weeds and rocks, dig some gravel and sand such as that which you can find on gravel bars inside creek bends or in the bedrock of the creek, and submerge the pan in the water. Then start swishing the water in a rotating motion. Let some of the water and sand spill out. Pick out the rocks and keep rotating the pan. Add more water, if needed. Soon you will have only black sand and small gravel. Add more water, swish it around, and tip it toward you. Hopefully some gold particles will stay in the bottom as the water and sand flow out.

A great deal of gold has been found on the Rogue River, either by wet-suited divers or Oregonians who work the banks after the high water has receded.

If you're serious about gold panning, you might want to read Verne Ballantyne's *How & Where to Find Gold* or John N. Dwyer's *Summer Gold, A Camper's Guide to Amateur Prospecting.*

A camera is a wonderful companion on a trip. Imagine yourself as Ansel Adams or Elliot Porter, and photograph the riverbed rocks, a rosy sunset, some unusual wild flowers, or a giant redwood. The results will bring back wonderful memories in years to come.

If you are the least bit artistic, take along a small sketch book and a pen or drawing pencil and make quick sketches of the scenic wonders. There are even tiny paint boxes available that will fit in your fishing vest pocket.

Armed with a pocket paperback, you might indulge in another pastime—identifying local wildflowers, birds, and trees. Evie's daughter Betsy presses her favorite leaves or flowers from fishing trips in a book. You can always make a mixed bouquet of flowers and grasses for the dining table at camp. And think of all the new birds you can identify. Roger Tory Peterson is *the* authority on birds and his guides are renowned. There's also *The Bird Watcher's Bible* by George Laycock, *The Audubon Society Field Guide to North American Birds,* or *Golden Guide to Field Identification of Birds of North America* by Chandler S. Robbins, Bertel Bruun, and Herbert Zim.

For help with familiar-looking trees you can't identify by name, turn to either Simon and Schuster's thick green volume *Guide to Trees* or Golden Press's *A Guide to Identification of Trees of North America.* There are so many wildflower books that it's difficult to single out any in particular, but the Peterson Field Guide Series, paperbacks that are keyed to a specific geographic area, are good and easy to use.

Many books have been written about edible wild foods, such as Euell Gibbons's *Stalking the Wild Asparagus.* Take a hike and gather wild asparagus, dandelion greens, watercress, and milkweed. Using one of the many books available, collect, sample, smell, and enjoy. But be very careful in your tasting and be sure that you can identify your wild food before you taste it. Be especially cautious with mushrooms. Once you have a bit of research behind you, wild foraging can be a wonderful hobby.

When the fish aren't biting, you can practice your casting. A goal of more accuracy and distance may pay off dividends. If you're learning to cast, a hint here and there from more experienced casters may make a big difference.

If you are with a native of the area, encourage him or her to tell you about the local history of the area and to identify trees, wildflowers, and birds. You may be lucky enough to see feeding deer, playful beavers, or wandering bears.

If it's exercise you're after, there's always jogging or hiking along the trails. Excursions to deserted recluses' cabins may unearth marvelous treasures of old bottles, cooking utensils, and handmade tools.

Are you a latent poet or essayist? If so, find a beautiful secluded place along the river and describe the peaceful scene spread out before you. Give a detailed account of the unique cloud formations, the intense colors in the sky, the shades of green of the trees, and the varieties of birds and wild flowers. In years to come it will be even more meaningful than your photographs or diary.

While observing nature, have you ever noticed the different animal tracks along the river banks and on the trails? Spotting a familiar track will make you feel more a part of nature and less alone. We're all familiar with the deer's hoof prints. Because deer are so shy you're more apt to see their tracks than the deer themselves. Their trails often lead to water; after they have grazed on grass, shrubs, and small trees, deer need a drink. The white-tail, blacktail, and mule deer usually travel in family groups and are a delight to watch.

Along the river banks you will often see otter and beaver tracks. The otter, a member of the weasel family, has five webbed toes. He is a superb swimmer and feeds on crayfish, fish, frogs, etc. You can recognize his tracks by the slide marks with footprints at each end. A helpful book is *A Field Guide to Animal Tracks* by Olaus J. Murie.

The beaver, a rodent, is an aquatic engineer best known for his dams made of sticks, logs, and mud. The beaver spends most of its time in the water but gathers food off the bark of the alder and poplar trees on the land. On the Boulder River in Montana a family of beavers built a dam more than seven feet high—a great engineering feat.

You may also notice rabbit tracks. Or raccoon tracks, with their long-nail foot marks. Other small animals you're apt to run across are the grey squirrel, woodchuck, skunk, muskrat, and porcupine.

Bear tracks are easy to identify because of their large size and shape. Bears are enthusiastic berry eaters but will also feed on fish and fresh meat. And near civilization they make excellent garbage collectors!

The animals you will spot will depend a great deal on the part of the country and type of terrain where you are fishing. The farther back in the wilderness you venture, the more unique animals you will meet. You might want to consult *Wildlife in America* by Peter Matthiessen.

Fortunately, there won't be too many days when the fish aren't biting or at least promising to bite. All fishermen have an irrepressibly optimistic attitude and can often be heard muttering, "Wait until tomorrow."

Wet Girl and Dry Girl

15

There is a continuing debate in fly fishing circles about the relative merits of the wet fly and the dry fly, but very little discussion concerning the differing characteristics of a wet and a dry girl.

Jane was an incurable dry girl—a bridge player and a golfer—whose idea of roughing it was to eat a sandwich on the front porch. She wore crisp white skirts topped by pale polyester blouses, and every blond hair on her head was arranged with calculated perfection. Dreading all things unsanitary, she spent twenty percent of her life in her clean-tiled bathroom. To her, camping was like serving a sentence on Devil's Island. Jane's wilderness was an apartment house swimming pool. Her summer tan was gold and even, like a carefully turned fried chicken.

Phoebe, on the other hand, was a wet girl: a backpacker, a wildflower-watcher, and a good camp cook. She looked her best in Levi's and faded cotton shirts. Her short black hair was tousled and casual, and sometimes she tied it with an old red bandanna. Phoebe liked to walk in the rain and swim in rivers. Her summer tan was not bikini-perfect because she couldn't resist wearing walking shorts and hiking boots. Her nose was often sunburned.

In spite of their differences, Phoebe and Jane were good friends, and their husbands shared an almost neurotic enthusiasm for fly fishing. The two women began to fear the dreadful possibility that they might have to spend their vacations at home alone while their husbands went off to the wilderness with that horrible, legendary group known as "The Boys." A quick counterattack had to be organized to combat the subtle charms of this poker-playing, duck-hunting, fly-fishing, closed fraternity. They devised a plan called "Operation Motel Fishing" and presented it to their husbands. The plan was to go, by station wagon, to Montana and Wyoming (that Mecca of all American fly fishermen), the land of the Continental Divide and birthplace of famous rivers— The Beaverhead, the Gallatin, the Yellowstone, the Big Hole, the Madison, the Boulder, the Green, and the Snake. All four of them would stay in comfortable motels near the great rivers; Jane could rough it in the sanitary confines of her antiseptic accommodations, Phoebe could plunge herself into America's famous rivers, and the husbands could wallow in the delights of fisherman's paradise. The last and most important part of the plan came as a surprise to the men when Phoebe and Jane said "Please, will you teach us how to fish?" (definitely a good ploy in combating the pull of "The Boys").

The three months preceding the motel-hopping trip were filled with instruction in knot tying, flycasting, fish and fly identification, and water reading. Jane's golfing friends were amazed to see her flycasting on one of the fairways. Jane's timing was superb and soon she was casting a long, lovely line. Phoebe attended a fly tying class at the local junior college and, with the aid of Art Flick's and Jack Dennis's splendid fly tying manuals, was soon tying a creditable assortment of Montana and Wyoming flies: Goofus Bugs, Joe's Hoppers, Renegades, Big Hole Demons, and Montana Stone Nymphs.

As all fishermen do, the husbands had collected masses of equipment— so there were rods, reels, and fly boxes for everybody. The only gear that Jane and Phoebe had to buy were waders and vests, which, when donned, made them look and feel like self-contained little robots. Jane was delighted to see how smashing she looked in Levi's. The husbands took their students on a preliminary "shakedown" fishing weekend to a small hatchery-stocked stream so they could experience the feel of striking and netting an actual trout.

The trip was planned for the last two weeks in August and the first

81

week in September. The American Automobile Association supplied the group with complete, detailed maps of their entire route and a tour book listing names, addresses, and telephone numbers of recommended motels.

Driving toward Montana through Idaho, they followed the great Snake River through the desert to its source in Yellowstone Park. They stopped to fish at Henry's Fork and the Gallatin. At first only the husbands landed any of the big, handsome browns and rainbows that inhabit these big streams; but by the time they reached Livingston and the Yellowstone, the wives were also catching trout.

They stayed at Old Faithful Inn in Yellowstone Park and were amazed to find fat, healthy trout thriving in the river, not far from the famous geyser. They read, with fascination, Charles Brooks's *The Trout and the Stream* (not only a fine instruction book for advanced fishermen but also an interesting account of the geographical, chemical, and geological makeup of certain rivers in the Yellowstone area).

They haunted the famous fishing and sporting goods stores, where the salespeople were all very helpful and fine fishermen, ready to give expert advice on guide service, stream conditions, and types of tackle needed. Phoebe, who had tied many of her own flies, was enchanted to see fifteen women at Dan Bailey's, sitting in little cubicles, leaning over vises, and speedily winding waxed thread, fur, and feathers into beautiful fishing flies (Bailey's catalogue lists hundreds of different patterns, which can be shipped to any place in the world).

All four fishermen thrived on the vacation. The husbands were really proud of their wives and began to view them not only as spouses but also as interesting fishing companions. They were four traveling fish enthusiasts, not just sightseeing tourists. One rainy evening, as they were returning to the motel for a hot shower, they passed a group of "The Boys" camped along the edge of a river. "The Boys" were having difficulty lighting their fire and seemed disenchanted by the leaking tent. Phoebe and Jane winked at each other like two old conspirators.

The last stop on the trip was Dillon, Montana, conveniently close to the Beaverhead and the Big Hole. Now, Dame Juliana Berners, extolling the peripheral joys of fishing in her fifteenth-century treatise by praising the sweet meadow flowers and the young swan and coot, had never been to Dillon; but if she had, she would have undoubtedly agreed that pulling into a Montana town on the eve of a rodeo weekend is certainly a peripheral joy on a fishing trip.

Dillon was full of handsome, lean cowboys in Stetson hats and high-heeled boots. A banner strung across the entrance to town read "Welcome to the biggest weekend in Montana." The windows of the Sundowner Motel, which was to be the group's home for the week, were painted with Wild West scenes and slightly risqué slogans. Phoebe's window sported a picture of a snorting Longhorn beside a sign that said "Horny Steer Saloon." Jane's room proclaimed itself to be "Off limits to the U.S. Cavalry." There were red and blue ladies, in various stages of undress, painted under this message.

Saturday dawned warm and sunny—not a good day for fishing but perfect for a rodeo. Sitting in the grandstand, the four fishermen watched cowboys perform back-breaking feats. Miss Montana Rodeo rode with an enviable grace, and a free barbecue was served to everyone present. Then the whole town exploded into a wild celebration of its western roots, ringing with revelry for three days and nights.

The final river to be fished was the Beaverhead. Two young guides floated the foursome downstream, showing them how to cast rubber-legged Girdle Bugs close to the grassy, brushy banks of the food-filled river. The Beaverhead was the fishiest river any of them had ever seen, full of fat, heavy brown trout and rainbows. They returned to this river again and again, sometimes with guides, sometimes with an intelligent young high school teacher—a knowledgeable conservationist and quite a fine fisherman.

On their last day in Dillon, it rained—this was the kind of day that a fisherman prays for. Even Jane, by now hopelessly hooked on fishing, came out from behind her racily painted windows wearing waders, rain jacket, and a smile.

A Hint a Day

16

Our society admires shortcuts, tips, and great little tricks. Women eagerly read Heloise's daily column for suggestions on how they can save five precious minutes with her clever ideas. Surely we need a Heloise of the fishing world to offer us this same useful service. But until she comes along, here are a few random thoughts that may help until you start developing your own bright ideas.

One of the best tools you can take with you are surgical forceps. Doctors use these to clamp veins while operating. As a fisherman, you will find these forceps essential for removing deeply embedded hooks in a fish's gullet or throat. If you plan to release the fish, it has a better chance of surviving if you've used the forceps. Attach the forceps to your fishing vest and you may be mistaken for a female Dr. Welby.

Another helpful gadget on the river is a nail clipper, tied to your vest. You'll need it every time you change your flies, cut leaders, and trim knots. These clippers also come with a needle at one end. This is essential for cleaning out the eyes of flies as well as loosening wind knots on your leader.

Some Kleenex stored in your vest is excellent to dry your fly before adding floatant.

Many fishermen feel more secure when wading if they carry a staff. This can be anything from a discarded ski pole, a sturdy stick found on the river bank, or a metal pole that collapses when not in use.

A helpful idea when you hook your fly on a nearby willow, rock, or log is to cast a loop of your line past this obstruction and then make a quick back cast to free your fly.

It's a good idea to frequently check your leader for wind knots (knots accidently formed while casting) and your hooks for bends or broken-off barbs. The "big one" may break your leader, if the leader has a wind knot. And you diminish your chances of landing a fish if you're using a bent or barbless hook.

When setting up your rod, double up your fly line before putting it through the rod guides so that the line won't slip back through the guides.

What a timesaver this can be; and by doing it you'll look like a pro!

Here's some advice for anglers bothered by insects. Light colors, such as tan, white, or pastels, are less attractive to bugs than dark colors. Black flies especially like dark colors and will bite right through a cotton shirt. So dress accordingly and bring lots of insect repellent. Recommended are those that have a high percentage of DEET (N-diethyl-meta-tolnamide).

While walking through dense and bushy woods, carry your rod in reverse, with the tip behind you. This will save you many tangles and protect the rod's delicate tip. After you've fished a while, you will realize why fishermen consider their rods sacred as well as precious.

John and Clara were fishing in Canada on their honeymoon. John had presented Clara with a delicate and valuable Hardy rod as a wedding present. As a new fisherman, she was only mildly impressed. One day, while fishing a turbulent stream she lost her balance and footing and was falling into the water. "Be careful of the rod," John shouted. "Keep it in the air." But it was too late, and Clara fell in. She managed to wade out and was thoroughly drenched. It can now be told . . . the only thing that saved their marriage was the unharmed rod!

Author Charles Brooks warns against keeping fish in the back pocket of your vest. He feels that the heat of your body cooks and spoils the fish. The few fish Wally keeps he puts in a plastic bag, which hangs by its string handles from the back of his vest. To keep the fish extra-fresh, he places ferns inside the bag. In New Zealand they use wild mint.

If you're fishing on a windy day, shorten your leader, make short casts, and always be sure to wear a hat and protective glasses. If the wind is blowing, try to position yourself so that the wind helps you. Don't fish with the sun in your eyes if you can possibly help it.

Polaroid glasses will not only help diminish sun problems but will also help you to see under the water so that you can spot fish, and to wade with greater safety.

Tape a big spring clamp to the handle of your net, just below where the net is attached. Gather your net and place the folds in the open clamp. Now it won't catch in the brush. When you want to net a fish, open the clamp with your thumb.

When fishing with weighted nymphs, tie a piece of bright-colored or luminous yarn around your leader at the middle barrel knot and at the butt. It will help you see the line when a fish strikes.

George Anderson suggests that sometimes fish will take one size larger fly than is on the river when there are lots of flies, since the more flies on the water, the more selective the fish are—and the larger fly will attract their

85

attention better.

If you are getting strikes but the fish seem to refuse at the last moment, try a smaller fly.

If a fish makes a splashy, splattering rise, it is probably chasing emerging nymphs, usually of Caddis Flies; so try a nymph just under the surface.

If you are fishing dry, try to have a fly you can see. One of the most visible, especially in the small sizes, is a Parachute Hackle tied with a white wing post.

You will find parachute flies most helpful as evening comes and darkness sets in.

For poor eyes, there are folding, magnifying glasses that attach permanently to the bill of your cap or hat.

When wading on a boat trip, to re-enter the boat, sit down and then swing your legs over the side. Wading boots were not designed for ballerinas.

Take two rods for the last hour of spring creek fishing to avoid retying different flies to your leader when it is getting dark and difficult to see.

If you are casting where there are a number of fish feeding, pick one fish and keep casting to it. Sooner or later he just may take it! If after five or six presentations the fish keeps refusing, change the pattern or size of your fly.

Mel Krieger urges us not to false cast directly over a fish. You'll spook him for sure!

Keep a notebook showing water conditions and insect hatches by dates. It will help you when you're planning future trips to the same stream.

When fishing the flat surface of a lake with no wind, try a dry fly using no motion, or a sunken nymph. With both, use long, light leaders.

Try to get into the best position to fish each spot instead of casting where you can't see well or where interfering currents will cause drag. In fast water, especially, you can get quite close without being seen. If you don't get close, it will be hard to fish without drag in fast water.

If you have your leader nail-knotted to your line, you can easily release a snagged hook by sliding the rod tip down the leader all the way to the fly.

A small sheath knife is much easier and quicker to use than a pocket knife.

Hooking your line with the fly is an annoyance that can be corrected by bringing your rod forward to the one o'clock position. Tip it ahead only at the end of the forward movement. If your line and leader pile up at the end of a cast, you are releasing the line too soon on the forward cast or exerting too much power at the end of the forward cast. To remedy this, release your line that you're holding in your left hand at the end of the forward movement and be sure to stop at the ten o'clock position. If you find you are snapping off your flies, perhaps you are starting your forward cast too soon or aren't giving the back cast enough force. The remedy is to watch your back cast and to only start casting forward when you see that the line and leader are out straight behind you. If you use enough power, the line will straighten out. Another mistake fishermen make is to tangle the rod with the fly. It's the same as wind knots . . . pushing the rod ahead after your tip has gone forward. Once again, stop the rod at the one o'clock position, have the tip come ahead last, and then let go of the line with your left hand. And should your line, leader, and fly slap down on the water enough to sink your dry fly, it's because you are bringing your forward cast too low. The cure is to aim your cast to stop two or three feet above the water. This will make your line land quietly on the water. Basically, if you think one o'clock and ten o'clock, a lot of your troubles will be solved.

And here is the last thing—if fishing is slower than you feel it should be, open up your next fish—assuming there is one—and examine what it's been eating. You may just be using the wrong fly.

17

Would You Want
Your Son to Marry A
Fisherman?

There's no question that we personally can answer this question with an enthusiastic "Yes." There are so many wonderful experiences to be savored when both members of a couple are anglers. There are trips to plan for, adventures to share, mishaps to laugh at, and memories to reminisce about.

Fishing together helps make each partner more understanding of the other's idiosyncrasies, as well. For example, Joe Cooper will not fish with a fly he has not tied himself. Most of the time he is a quiet, contemplative man who winds his treasured lures out of old muskrat fur, deer hair, and wood-duck feathers. Then, equipped with a heavy fly box containing hundreds of variations of both wet and dry fly patterns, he is a model of preparedness for almost any stream condition. This dedicated man has been known to let Gwen ride a boat through White Horse Rapids while he carried his fly box and rod down the safer trail.

Gwen had always feared that someday they would arrive at a river where the fish were refusing everything but Girdle Bugs, Rat-Faced Mac-Dougalls, or some other fly not in her husband's repertoire. Sure enough, her fears were realized when they arrived at a Montana fishing resort where men, women, and children were having unqualified success in attracting huge rainbows and brown trout with something called a Montana Stone Nymph. The fish seemed addicted to that one fly; they ignored everything that Joe presented from his fly box. His frustration was agonizing to watch. Generous children offered Montana Stone Nymphs from their own juvenile collections, but he declined, explaining that he never fished a fly he had not tied himself.

The next morning, a particularly sensitive child came to Joe's cabin, carrying a little vise, three bare-shanked hooks, a small roll of black chenille, a wad of yellow wool, and a few black hackle feathers—in all, the perfect gift for the suffering fisherman. Gratefully and fervently, Joe tied himself three Montana Stone Nymphs.

For the next few days he happily joined the frolicking anglers in the successful acquisition of big Boulder River trout. Then, as might be expected, he lost one of his Montana Stone Nymphs. Worry lines began to develop between his eyes, especially when the hook broke on his second fly. He didn't sleep well that night. The next day he cast the remaining fly carefully and only into calm, obstacle-free water; but on a hearty back cast he lodged his last Montana Stone Nymph in the tall branches of a cottonwood tree.

Gwen gasped fearfully. From a distance, she watched in horror as another intense fisherman handed her husband a pistol. Despairingly, she watched Joe disappear into the cottonwood. There was a single shot. Gwen cried out, "Dear Lord, he's killed himself." She didn't know whether to be angry or relieved when he reappeared, smiling like a reprieved convict, with the Montana Stone Nymph in his hand and a cottonwood twig in his hatband.

If your son does marry a woman fisherman, they may eventually have some small fry to bring along on their fishing excursions. At first they may just go to lakes and rivers, but later they can pack into woodland and mountain streams. Imagine the fun of raising your own fishing companions.

Joe Cooper wasn't one to let his own purist tendencies interfere with his objective of teaching his children to fish. Since a child gets easily discouraged by long waits without a strike, scrappy little panfish are the most accommodating for these beginning anglers, and a fat red worm is the closest thing to a sure-fire lure.

Joe was able to turn even the first simple excursions to Clear Lake—when the children still carried their teddy bears and security blankets along with their lunch, bamboo poles, and personally dug worms—into a fantastic adventure. And since yarn spinning is such an integral part of fishing, he told them all about the disreputable Fish-gut Pete—a fish-gutter by profession who smelled so horrible that his wife wouldn't even let him in the house. The children, of course, warmed up right away to Pete's untidiness; so Joe made good use of Pete to teach his kids the proper, slow, sidearm swing they needed to cast a worm, and the correct way to strike and play the scrappy little bluegills, sunfish, crappies, and perch they fished for. And it was Fish-gut Pete who chided them if they were squeamish about baiting their hooks or cleaning their fish.

This worked well, and today the two no-longer children still share their father's enthusiasm for fishing. Marky lives in England where she finds rare old books for Joe's fishing library. On a recent Christmas she sent Fish-gut Pete an antique walnut fly box containing, in one of its cork-lined drawers, two beautifully tied Jock Scott salmon flies.

Gwen, the fourth Cooper to become an angler, got involved only after her children were grown; but Evie and Wally were fortunate enough to share the joy of fishing with their three children, and of introducing them to the wilderness. At first, they focused on making sure the children caught fish, so they would be more encouraged to go on. Betsy hooked her first while she was soaking her leader. One well-remembered family trip was to "Limit" Lake, where young Wally caught—and released—fifty-nine cutthroat trout that ran from eight to twelve inches. The trips were a perfect way to spend some uninterrupted days with the children and some of their friends.

But fishing with children has a wider reach than merely family excursions. For the past ten years there has been a program called the San Francisco Police Fishing Program, which encourages and stimulates freshwater and saltwater fishing among the youth of the city. Its many pluses include off-duty police officers teaching youngsters to fish, establishing a better police-youth relationship. Through the generosity of many businessmen, civic leaders, and citizens, a worthy delinquency prevention program has been brought about. Many similar programs are now in existence in other cities throughout the country.

Fishing has potential for enriching ordinary traveling either as a couple or a family. Sooner or later the mind rebels at traditional tourist attractions, and that's the time to dig out the fishing gear from the bottom of the suitcase. Evie advocates packing a small five-piece rod, a reel, and a few favorite flies when she travels. Two of her most memorable tourist fishing experiences were on the Rijeka River in Yugoslavia and in Kashmir, India. What better way to meet the people of another country than by sharing a common pursuit?

The adventure in Yugoslavia occurred as Evie and Wally were driving toward Plitvice National Parks, a geological wonder of sixteen lakes connected by superb falls. The land reminded them of Maine or Oregon. The beautiful stream that darted, snakelike, in and out along the route tantalized them into conjuring up private fantasies of a "big one" resting in a cool, deep hole, just waiting to be challenged by their expertly cast fly. They decided to take a romantic side trip and stopped at the next town for a loaf of newly-baked bread, a slab of local cheese, and a bottle of *vin de pays*—and to make inquiries of the hotel manager.

As if by magic, he produced the village's leading fisherman who, sensing their interest and enthusiasm, gave up his lunch hour to take them to his own favorite pool. Fish were breaking water and feeding all around as Evie assembled her rod. She cast to where she'd seen some boils in the water and felt a few nudges on the fly. The fish were not only there but eager, too; so she cast again—and the inevitable happened. The fly found a new home in a nearby willow tree. While it was being retrieved, the delicate rod broke. The fishing came to an abrupt halt.

Another time, on an angling side-trip in New Delhi, Evie learned that all the fishing rules she'd been taught and observed over the years were either ignored or reversed in the Vale of Kashmir. They bought licenses and then it was necessary to rent a "beat" (a stretch of river) and line up some gillies or "shifaris" who would be the guides. "Watchers" would observe the fishing, patrolling the assigned river to ensure that the licensed anglers didn't exceed their limit, that there were no poachers, and that natives didn't dynamite the rivers for food.

The three-hour drive from Srinagar to the mountain rivers and back to Srinagar was as exciting and colorful as the fishing. The drivers, who must have been related to reckless-driver Barney Oldfield, used their horns instead of their brakes. The noisy blasts scattered dogs, children, goats, sheep, bullocks, and horse-drawn carts as the drivers tore through each village. The Haas's saw miles and miles of terraced rice paddies, filled with working families, before they finally arrived at a twisting, turbulent river where two tall, slim Indian gillies waited.

These two spoke only a few words of English. Communications evolved into a kind of charade. The Indian gillies immediately set up the rods, then tied on those flies that they felt would be successful. When they realized that "the woman" was to fish also, they were not overjoyed.

The rods that the gillies supplied were made of glass, and the level line was greatly worn and rough. The flies were large and colorful and not like any Evie had seen before. The gillies added a metal weight to the leader, between the two flies. The Indians could hardly wait until the fishermen put on their rubber boots. Immediately, the guides dashed across the road to the river, pointed to a bubbling pool, and motioned them to cast. But, unhappy with the Westerners' casting performance, they took the rods and cast upstream and let the fly float downstream in the turbulent water. Evie and Wally expected the gillies to retrieve the line then; but instead they dragged the fly across the current and upstream. Dragging a fly upstream has always been frowned on—a real "no-no." But eventually, fish were caught in this manner. The fish were brown trout, planted years ago by the British when they governed India and controlled the rivers. Both Evie and Wally had many strikes, which proved that the river was teaming with fish. The high waters made the fishing unusual. It was a mystery how fish could rest in such raging, wild water—or how these fish could spot the fly.

The gillies worked hard all day. They leapt from rock to rock with the agility of mountain goats. If a fly was caught on a submerged rock or branch, they waded barefoot to the spot and carefully retrieved the fly. When wading was too difficult, each insisted that his fisherman climb on his back and be piggy-backed across the river. At the end of the day, the tip was twenty rupees or $2.60 . . . and that was considered generous. One will forever wonder what the fishing would have been like with adequate rod, line, and flies.

These are only a smattering of the experiences that inspire the authors to answer with an emphatic "Yes" when asked, "Would you want your son to marry a fisherman?" Fishing is simply a good thing to do together. We hope that by now, this "why-to" text has prompted you to follow the footsteps of Dame Juliana, Carrie Stevens, Louise Brewster Miller, Joan Wulff, and Mary Rentschler. Mary Rentschler belongs to the Woman Flyfishers Club, an organization of more than eighty-five devoted female fishing enthusiasts. Founded in 1932, this club has a clubhouse on the west branch of the Neversink River in New York State and is dedicated to the enjoyment of fishing and the preservation of "the beautiful and valuable heritage of our world."

Fish in the Pan and Other Ways, Too

18

B y now, you must realize that we advocate "catch and release" fishing.
And because we also admire freshly caught fish as food, we advocate
doing culinary justice to a reasonable portion of the catch.

Freshly caught fish always tastes best eaten on the river; but whatever
you plan for the fish you keep, clean them as soon as possible after you
catch them and keep them cool until you cook them.

To clean a fish, insert a sharp knife in the anal vent and cut toward the head and tip of the lower jaw, splitting the fish wide open. Then make a second cut, crosswise, to sever the connection between jaw (and gills) and the body. Remove the gills and entrails by spreading the body walls apart and cutting free any connecting tissue. To complete the cleaning, hold the fish by the jaw with one hand and pull out the gill section and intestines with the other. With your thumb, scrape off the layer of blood lying against the spine and thoroughly rinse the fish.

Obviously, refrigeration is desirable—but it's not always available. Lacking a refrigerator, ice, or chemical ice pack, you can keep your fish cool and fresh for a reasonable time wrapped in damp grass, moss, wild mint, or newspaper.

To do freshly caught fish gourmet justice, bring along a pan, as well as some flour in a brown paper bag in which to shake the cleaned, washed catch. Shake the fish in the flour; remove the excess; add salt and pepper; and place it in a skillet bubbling with a generous mixture of half butter and half oil or margarine (all-butter can cause a burnt flavor). Sauté the fish until it is nicely brown on one side; then turn it and cook it on the other side. When it flakes, it is done. No fork is necessary—enjoy it corn-on-the-cob style.

Wally skins his trout (skinning must be done while the fish is fresh) before he fries it. The Japanese, who prize the skin, would not approve.

You don't need to carry a pan to cook your fresh catch in the woods. Steam it in aluminum foil that you've carried in your creel. If you are far-sighted, you'll even have brought along some salt and pepper, a lemon, a slice or two of bacon or some butter, and maybe even a tomato. Salt and pepper the fish inside and out and then put the butter or bacon and tomato in the cavity. Secure the foil tightly by crimping the edge, place the packet in hot coals, and cover it with more coals. A twelve-inch trout cooks in about twenty minutes. The larger the fish, the longer the cooking time. It will taste better than any fish served in the fanciest restaurant.

New Zealanders, after starting the campfire and while waiting for the coals to glow, wrap freshly caught trout tightly in single sheets of very wet newspaper. They use six or seven sheets, wrapping the fish separately in each sheet. Then they put the packets on top of some green branches and place them on hot coals. They make sure to turn the fish every few minutes to keep the paper from burning too quickly. Gradually, the paper burns away, leaving only two layers—which, at last, open and separate from the fish. Eureka! The fish is cooked, removed from the fire, served and enjoyed. In Chile the fish is salted, peppered, and buttered. Then it is wrapped in wax paper, then in wet newspaper, and cooked in very hot embers for ten minutes.

Still another unique method of cooking is to wrap trout in corn husks and cook over the coals. Season inside and outside of cleaned fish with salt and pepper. Rub inside of fish with butter. Slit corn husk down one side and take out silk. If fish is too large cut off head and tail. Take out the ear of corn and put one fish inside each husk. Tie the husk closed in several places and soak in water for a few minutes. Place wet husk on low coals and roast for 8 to 12 minutes. Cook them first on one side. Turn and cook for several minutes on the other side. Fish can be served in husks.*

Another novel way to cook trout on a fishing trip is to skewer it on sticks and dip it in barbecue sauce. Make the following barbecue sauce, pack it in a clean coffee can, and seal it tightly with freezer tape.

Barbecue Sauce One

1 cup tomato juice	Worcestershire
⅔ cup butter or	sauce
margarine (or half	1 teaspoon chili
of each combined)	powder
1 cup white wine (dry)	1 teaspoon paprika
2 tablespoons brown	¼ teaspoon pepper
sugar	1 small onion chopped
4 tablespoons cider	small
vinegar	1 clove garlic minced
1½ teaspoons salt	(optional)
1 teaspoon	

Simmer the above for ten minutes and use this sauce for your cleaned trout, which are skewered on strong green sticks or long-handled forks. Dip frequently to keep fish moist and cook fish for approximately 10 to 15 minutes over low coals.**

Barbecue Sauce Two

Here's a simpler barbecue sauce recipe. You can use it as a dip

---

*This recipe used by permission of *Sunset Magazine.*
**This recipe used by permission of *Sunset Magazine.*

for skewered fish, or as a sauce.

¼ cup corn oil	¾ cup water
¼ cup cider vinegar	3 drops Tabasco sauce
1 cup catsup	1 teaspoon chili
⅓ cup Worcestershire	powder
sauce	2 teaspoons salt

Be sure to salt and pepper the inside of the fish. Bake a one-pound fish for fifteen minutes, a two-pound fish for twenty-five minutes, and a three-pound fish for thirty-five minutes.

Dutch-Oven Trout

Cooking trout in a Dutch oven is another easy and delicious way to prepare your catch. Place the fish in the Dutch oven with an eighth-pound of butter. Cover with oven lid and put on top of a hot bed of coals. For more even heat, you can put coals on the lid as well. Eighteen minutes later, the fish will be ready to eat. There will be no need to turn it during the cooking.

Plank-Cooked Fish

Another unusual method of cooking fish in the woods is to use a hardwood plank. First heat the plank in front of a bed of coals until it is sizzling hot. Split the belly of the fish and clean it. Then tack your fish, skin side down, to the plank with nails and prop it up in front of the fire. Baste with butter, oil, or margarine, and turn the plank upside down. When the fish is flaky it is done. Salt and pepper to taste.

Whether you cook outdoors or indoors, the basic guidelines for cooking fish are the same. Don't overcook—stop while the fish is moist and flaky. A delicate sauce is ideal; if you use too heavy a hand with the condiments, you could easily lose the unique taste of a freshly caught fish.

A chilled dry white wine such as a Riesling or Pinot Blanc or Chardonnay is an ideal complement to fish. Add a crisp salad, some wild watercress, thinly sliced cucumbers or sweet, firm, red tomatoes, and you have perfect companions for your fish. If you aren't too calorie-conscious, include some toasted French bread or hot corn bread and honey. In any case, the fish will be the star attraction of the meal, especially if it's newly caught.

Minted Trout

Zane Gray liked to cook his trout in mint leaves. After cleaning his brookie, he sprinkled it with a teaspoon each of salt and pepper. He then marinated the fish for an hour (or longer) in one tablespoon of lemon juice, two tablespoons of olive oil, one tablespoon of thyme, and six sprigs of fresh mint. He placed his fish on a grill over hot coals and cooked it for twenty minutes, turning and basting the fish frequently.

Orcus Island Salmon

Our friend Dee tells of an Indian tribe living on the beach in the Orcus Islands who, in cooking salmon, improvise on the traditions of their fathers and grandfathers. They season the cavity of an eight-pound fish and wrap the fish securely in chicken wire, fastening the ends—which they then use as handles. Dee, who has since tried this method of cooking a large fish, has found it to be a great hit with her guests. In the cavity she puts bay leaves, sliced onion, celery leaves, white pepper, and slices of lemon. Before wiring the fish she sprinkles it inside and out with lemon and white vermouth. The fish is cooked for fifteen to twenty minutes on each side and is basted occasionally with wine. When the wire is removed, the skin sticks to the wire and the fish pulls away from the backbone to fillet itself.

Not all trout, steelhead, salmon, etc. are cooked in the woods. You can be more elaborate and impressive if you cook in your very own kitchen. Here, assisted by assorted herbs and your chopping board, you can create great culinary experiences. We'd like to share with you some of our favorite recipes.

Chinese-Style Trout (to cook six medium-sized trout)

Marinate cleaned fish in a shallow pan with the following mixed ingredients:

½ cup sherry
3 tablespoons salad oil
¼ cup (4 tablespoons)
  soy sauce
2 tablespoons lime
  juice (fresh or

bottled)
1 tablespoon brown
  sugar
¼ teaspoon dry ginger
  (freshly ground or
  powdered)

Leave fish in marinade for 2 hours in the refrigerator. Meanwhile, toast over low heat in a frying pan 2 tablespoons of sesame seeds. They should be golden in about 3 minutes.

Drain off marinade and bake fish in a moderately hot oven (375°) for about 20 minutes or until fish is flaky. Using your marinade occasionally baste fish and turn it during the cooking. Before serving sprinkle with sesame seeds.

This recipe can be used for broiled or barbecued fish as well.*

Teriyaki Trout or Salmon (for four people)

For lovers of fish cooked Japanese-style on skewers, here are two versions of this recipe.

Japanese Version:

4 fillets of fresh trout,
  or the fillet of
  salmon cut into 4
  pieces
3 tablespoons soy
  sauce

4 teaspoons sake *or*
  mirin (a sweet kind
  of sake) *or* honey *or*
  sweet sherry
1 teaspoon cornstarch

Hawaiian Version:

4 fillets of fresh trout
  or salmon, as above
½ cup soy sauce
2 tablespoons brown

sugar
1 teaspoon cornstarch
2 tablespoons white
  wine

Place soy sauce and mirin (or sherry, sake, or honey) into a saucepan and boil it until it reduces to thirty percent of its original amount. In a separate dish, add a small amount of water to the cornstarch to form a paste. Combine with soy mixture. Cook until the sauce thickens and clears.

---

*This recipe used by permission of *Sunset Magazine.*

Put fish on greased metal skewers, using two skewers for each piece of fish. You may, if you prefer, use a metal grill in place of skewers. If you do, be sure that it is oiled so that the fish won't stick to it. Grill the fish on both sides, until it is nicely browned, then heavily brush on the *teriyaki mixture* (whether the Japanese or Hawaiian version). Grill lightly once more and baste again with the sauce. Keep alternating grilling and basting at least four or five times. Keep the heat low—teriyaki burns easily and tastes bad when scorched.

Foil-Baked Trout or Salmon

The Japanese also bake their trout fillets or salmon steak in foil. They put one tablespoon of sake or dry sherry and four slices of lemon onto each well-salted and-peppered fish. You can also include a little butter with each fish.

Sashimi

Sashimi, a delicious appetizer, is made of sliced, raw fish. Only sea-going fish are safe to eat. Tuna, steelhead, and salmon—if freshly caught—will do fine.

raw fish, sliced slantwise 1½ inches wide and ¼ inch thick	daikon (Japanese radish)
carrots, thinly sliced	myoga ginger
	parsley
	lettuce

Cut the fish as indicated above. Place the slices on a serving platter so that they overlap. Use any or all of the remaining ingredients as a garnish. Dip into the sauce (recipe below) and eat along with the fish.

Sashimi Dipping Sauce

A shashimi dipping sauce is always served with the raw fish slices. The sauce can be storebought—Kikkoman has a prepared sashimi sauce—or homemade.

For the latter, mix:

½ cup soy sauce	mustard
1 teaspoon dry	1 teaspoon water

**For a more traditional
sauce, mix:**

¼ cup soy sauce   **wasabi powder.**
1 teaspoon (or more)

Wasabi powder is horseradish powder, and it is very sharp, indeed.

Ceviche

There is also a raw fish appetizer from Spain—*Ceviche*. For approximately one pound of trout, cut into small pieces, add the following ingredients:

½ small onion, finely
  chopped
⅛ cup chopped green
  peppers or part of a
  small can of green

chilies (to taste)
3 tablespoons olive oil
1 cup fresh lemon
  juice or ¾ cup fresh
  lime juice

Pour this mixture over the fish and refrigerate for at least four hours. The fish should marinate and be served in a glass, china, or pottery dish.

Graulax, or Salted Salmon

Graulax, or salted salmon, is another way to serve raw fish. It can be offered as an appetizer or part of a smorgasbord.

To begin this dish, remove the head and tail from a 10-pound salmon, split it lengthwise, and take out the center bone. With a tweezer remove the small bones from the two fillets. Arrange the fillets, skin side down, in 2 shallow pans. Sprinkle each one with 3 tablespoons salad oil and 1 teaspoon each of salt, sugar, and coarsely ground white pepper. Cover the fillets completely with sprigs of fresh dill and sprinkle each fillet with 1 tablespoon brandy. Put a heavy weight on each fillet to press it evenly. Marinate the weighted fillets in a cool place for 1 to 2 days, but do not refrigerate them. Drain off the liquid and reserve 2 tablespoons.

Make mustard sauce: In a bowl combine ¾ cup mayonnaise, 6 tablespoons Düsseldorf mustard, the reserved liquid from the salmon, and 2 tablespoons sugar and beat the mixture thoroughly. Stir in 2 tablespoons chopped dill and pour the sauce into a sauceboat.

Transfer the salmon fillets to a board and with a very sharp knife slice them thinly at an angle. Serve the salmon with the mustard sauce. The salmon will keep refrigerated for 1 week.*

There are several sauces that you can serve with this fish.

Green Mayonnaise

This sauce is good with cold salmon and trout.

To 2 cups mayonnaise add 2 tablespoons minced parsley, 1 tablespoon snipped chives, 1 tablespoon minced fresh tarragon or ½ teaspoon dried, 1 teaspoon snipped dill, and 1 teaspoon minced fresh chervil or ¼ teaspoon dried.*

Mix together and let stand for two hours in refrigerator. Serve cold.

Sauce Verte

This is another and more elaborate version of green mayonnaise. (You'll need a ten-pound salmon.)

2 quarts homemade mayonnaise	**sieved**
2 bunches watercress (leaves only)	**2 tablespoons Grey's Poupon Mustard**
1 bunch parsley, minced (head only)	**2 tablespoons Gulden's Mustard**
4 tablespoons hard-boiled egg yolk,	**dash of white vinegar**
	juice of 1 lemon

Watercress Mayonnaise

Here's another sauce that's a winner with cold fish.

In a blender blend 1½ cups mayonnaise, ¾ cup chopped watercress leaves, 1 tablespoon snipped dill, and 1 teaspoon each of lemon juice and grated onion until the mixture is evenly colored, and add lemon juice, salt, and white pepper to taste.*

---

*This recipe used by permission of *Gourmet Magazine.*

Mustard Sauce

Combine in a bowl:

¾ cup mayonnaise	mustard
4 tablespoons Dijon	3 tablespoons sugar
mustard	2 tablespoons dill,
1 teaspoon dry	chopped

For added flavor and to thin mixture, pour in a small amount of the liquid from the salmon. Mix well and serve cold with salmon.

Smoked Trout, Salmon, or Steelhead

On the Rogue River in Oregon, some friends have built a small smokehouse, in which they have had great success with their smoked steelhead. From the outside the smokehouse resembles a Chick Sale outhouse. It is a square building about the size of a small closet, with three sliding, chicken-wired shelves at the top half of the smokehouse. The ground level is used for making small fires of green madrone or other slow-burning wood.

If you live in the city and want a simpler method of smoking fish, invest in a portable Swedish fish smoker. This is small and can be used on your patio at home, in the fireplace, or even on the bank of the river. With the smoker comes a special mixture of sawdust, and the fire is heated by a can of Sterno. The regular smokehouse takes ten to twelve hours to smoke the fish properly but the portable smoker does the job in eight to ten minutes.

Before you start using either method to smoke the fish, you must treat the fish with a mixture of brown sugar and salt. Our Oregon friends clean and fillet their fish (leaving on the skin) and then rub on a half-and-half brown sugar and salt for large fish (they use less salt if the fish are small). Then the fish are stored overnight in a pan in the refrigerator. A brine will form and marinate the fish. The next morning, they wash the fish thoroughly to remove the salt and sugar and pat them dry. Then they place them, skin down, on the wire shelves and start the fire.

Our friends keep the fire low, so the fish are smoked gradually. Each hour, they watch the fire so that it will not go out. If the fish are extra-large, they will take longer to smoke. After the fish has cooled, our friends pack them in small bundles and freeze them for future treats.

If you want to smoke fish on the portable smoker, sprinkle an ounce or so of salt and brown sugar mixture on the trout and smoke it, skin down, as is. It can be eaten eight minutes later!

Smoked steelhead spread on crackers at cocktail time is a real treat. Mash and mix the fish with mayonnaise, lemon juice, and chopped parsley. Your guests will come back for more.

Poached Fish

One of the basic and most popular ways to cook large fish is to poach them. Cooked in this manner, steelhead and salmon are a great delicacy. A simple, foolproof court bouillon recommended by Emalee Chapman for poaching is as follows:

1 quart water	**1 bay leaf**
2 onions, sliced, or ¼	**1 tablespoon sea salt**
cup shallots	**pepper to taste**
1 pint white wine	**cloves, celery stalk,**
1 bunch parsley or	**or lemon slices**
dill	**(optional)**
thyme	

Add ingredients to water. Bring the court bouillon to a boil for half an hour and strain before adding the fish. Cook salmon or steelhead thirty to forty minutes (or eight minutes per pound) over a low flame so that the liquid barely simmers. The water should shiver, not bubble. Cover the fish with the liquid. Cool fish in liquid. If you do not have a poacher and rack, wrap fish in cheesecloth—it will be easier to manage. Leave loose ends for handles.

Mousseline Sauce

This hot sauce is a traditional accompaniment to poached fish. Fold two to four tablespoons of whipped cream into one cup of hollandaise.

Caper Sauce

3 tablespoons butter	**dill, chopped**
3 tablespoons flour	**juice of 1 lemon**
¾ cup cream	**salt and pepper to**
2 tablespoons capers	**taste**
1 tablespoon fresh	

Heat the butter in a pan. Gradually add the flour. Stir in the cream. Cook for ten to fifteen minutes and stir to keep from burning. When sauce is thick, remove from heat. Add capers, dill, lemon juice, salt, and pepper.

Baked Salmon, Trout, or Steelhead

One of the more delicious ways to cook fish is to bake it. Here are a few ideas.

For baked steelhead or salmon in white wine:

In a dish combine 2 tablespoons minced parsley, 1 teaspoon thyme, and ½ teaspoon marjoram. Rinse and dry the fish and sprinkle the skin and cavity with the herb mixture and salt and pepper to taste. Put the fish in a well-buttered gratin dish just large enough to hold it and dot it with ½ stick or ¼ cup butter, softened and cut into bits. Put the fish in a preheated hot oven (400°F.) until the butter is melted, sprinkle it with 2 tablespoons lemon juice, and bake it, brushing it twice with melted butter, for 15 minutes. Sprinkle the fish lightly with salt and broil it under a preheated broiler, brushing it once with butter, for 10 minutes, or until the skin is crisp and the fish flakes easily when tested with a fork. Transfer the fish with 2 slotted spoons to a heated serving platter and keep it warm.

Stir ¼ cup dry white wine into the pan juices, bring the liquid to a boil, and cook it for 5 minutes. Season the sauce with salt and pepper to taste, spoon some of it over the fish, and serve the remaining sauce in a sauceboat. Serves 4.*

Sauce One

For sauce stir a quarter-cup of dry white wine into the pan juices and bring liquid to boil. Cook for five minutes. Season with salt and pepper to taste. Pour some of the sauce over the fish and serve the rest of the sauce separately.

Sauce Two

For a richer, thicker sauce.

---

*This recipe used by permission of *Gourmet Magazine.*

⅓ cup clam juice or
  fish stock
⅓ cup white wine
¾ cup butter

(preferably sweet)
6 egg yolks
parsley, chopped
lemon wedges

Combine in a double boiler clam juice or fish stock, white wine, and butter. Cook until butter is melted. Add egg yolks, adding each separately and beating each well with a wire whisk. Continue to cook until sauce is as thick as cream. Spoon over the fish and serve. Sprinkle with parsley for color and taste, and garnish with lemon wedges.

Rosé Hollandaise Sauce

This is a delicate sauce.

4 egg yolks
½ cup butter, melted
1 tablespoon lemon

juice
¼ teaspoon salt
½ cup rosé wine

Mix the egg yolks and melted butter first, and then add the wine. To thicken, put in double boiler and stir constantly until smooth and thick. Remove from stove (and water) and add lemon and salt.

Hollandaise and Sour Cream Sauce

Here's another delicious form of hollandaise for baked or grilled fish.

1 cup hollandaise
  sauce
1 cup sour cream
1 teaspoon lemon
  juice
1 teaspoon
  horseradish
a pinch nutmeg,

grated, or dried
a pinch cayenne
pepper
2 tablespoons dry
sherry, brandy, or
sauterne wine
(optional)

In a double boiler (be sure water isn't too hot) combine hollandaise sauce and sour cream. Add lemon juice, horseradish, nutmeg, and cayenne pepper. Heat sauce until it's warm and, if you wish, add dry sherry, brandy, or sauterne wine.

Mousseline-Moutard Sauce

Here's another variation.

1½ cups hollandaise sauce	cream
3-4 tablespoons thick	Dijon mustard, to taste

Mix ingredients and serve.

Assorted Vegetables

Assorted vegetables make another delicious addition to a baked fish recipe.

2-3 tomatoes, sliced	salt and pepper to taste
1 slice onion	white wine (optional)
fresh mushrooms, chopped	shrimp and/or crab meat (optional)
parsley, chopped	Parmesan cheese, grated (optional)
lemons, chopped	
¾ -1 cup fish stock or clam juice	

Put your fish in a large baking dish and place on top of it the tomatoes, onion, mushrooms, parsley, and lemons. For moisture include the fish stock or clam juice. Salt and pepper to taste. Bake in 350° oven. If fish is two or three pounds, it will take thirty-five minutes. If larger, it will take up to one or one and a half hours. When it's flaky, it's done. Don't overcook or it will disintegrate. The fish can be basted with white wine. Shrimp and crab meat can be added near the end, and grated parmesan cheese can be sprinkled over the fish during the last ten minutes of cooking.

Stuffed Baked Fish

Baked fish may also be stuffed, and there are many variations, including these. Wash and dry the fish, and salt and pepper the cavity. Pack your stuffing lightly and skewer the opening to-gether. Vary the amount of stuffing according to the fish's size. Bake in a shallow buttered dish or on a cookie sheet covered with foil. For a large fish, bake fifteen minutes at 550° and then forty-five minutes at 450°. For a three-to-five pound fish, bake at 350° for thirty minutes.

Baked Fish Oyster Dressing (for six to eight people)

8 small oysters, chopped	3 tablespoons cream
¼ cup bread crumbs	1 tablespoon sherry
1 anchovy, chopped fine	3 egg yolks, beaten lightly
1 teaspoon parsley, chopped	4 tablespoons soft butter
1 teaspoon tarragon, chopped	salt and pepper to taste

Combine oysters, bread crumbs, anchovy, parsley, tarragon, cream, sherry, egg yolks, and butter. Mix thoroughly, stuff, and bake.

Mushroom Stuffing (for six to eight people)

½ onion, chopped	1 cup soft bread crumbs
5 or 6 fresh mushrooms, chopped	¼ cup dry wine
3 tablespoons butter	salt & pepper to taste
2 chives, cut finely	

Melt butter and simmer onions until you can see through them. Simmer mushrooms for a few minutes. Add bread crumbs, chives, wine, and seasoning. Mix well. Bake on baking sheet covered with foil in 350° oven for thirty minutes.

Shrimp and Wild Rice Stuffing (for six to eight people)

1 cup wild rice, cooked	2 tablespoons parsley, chopped
1 cup shrimp, cut up	2 tablespoons butter
1 teaspoon capers, chopped	salt and pepper to taste

107

Combine. Stuff fish and bake.

Herb Stuffing

1 shallot, chopped
1 teaspoon onion,
   chopped
1 cup bread crumbs,
   soaked in milk and
   squeezed dry
3 fresh mushrooms,
chopped
1 tablespoon each
   thyme, fennel,
   chopped chives
salt and pepper to
   taste

Cook shallot and onions for a few minutes. Add other ingredients and mix. Stuff and bake. As a variation, substitute two tablespoons of white wine in place of milk and add one to one and a half tablespoons of chopped, salted cashews to stuffing. When it is cooked, sprinkle with a mixture of two tablespoons chopped parsley and two tablespoons chopped cashews. Sprinkle the fish with paprika and decorate the platter with watercress and lemon wedges.

Grilled or Barbecued Salmon, Steelhead, or Trout

Thoroughly wash and dry the fish. Then rub it with lemon juice and softened butter or margarine. Be sure the grill is well greased to keep fish from sticking or falling apart. The fire should not be too hot. Cook skin side down until it turns pink. Flip over and broil other side to get a smoked flavor. The fish will be ready after four or five minutes of cooking on each side. Serve with lemon or dill butter.

Stuffed Trout in Paper

Put 3 cups finely chopped mushrooms, a handful at a time, in a cloth and twist it tightly to extract the moisture. In a skillet sauté 1 cup each of finely chopped onions and celery in ½ stick or ¼ cup butter and 2 tablespoons oil until the vegetables are tender. Add the mushrooms and cook the mixture over high heat, stirring, for 2 to 3 minutes, or until the moisture has evaporated and the mushrooms are cooked. Stir in 1½ teaspoons salt, ½ teaspoon thyme, and pepper to taste.

Clean and remove the backbone from 4 trout, each weighing ¾ pound. Stuff each trout with some of the vegetable mixture and sprinkle them with salt and pepper to taste. Brush the trout with melted butter and broil them about 3 inches from the heat for 4 minutes. Cut 4 heart-shaped pieces of cooking parchment paper, each large enough to hold one trout, and butter the paper. Put the trout in the center of the paper, fold the paper over the fish, and crimp the edges of the paper tightly together. Oil the paper, put the packets on an oiled cookie sheet, and bake them in a hot oven (425°F.) for about 15 minutes, or until the parchment is inflated and browned. Serves 4.*

Dill Butter

Snip finely enough dill to measure ¼ cup and in a bowl combine it well with 1½ sticks (¾ cup) butter, well softened, and lemon juice, salt, and pepper to taste. Spread the butter in a ½-inch layer in a dish and chill it for 1 to 2 hours, or until it is firm. With a small cutter cut the butter into stars or other decorative shapes and keep the cutouts chilled in a bowl of ice water. Let the butter soften to room temperature before serving.**

Trout Cooked in Beer One

The English and New Zealanders are fond of trout cooked in beer.

1 cup beer	6 peppercorns, whole
1 bay leaf	1 lemon, sliced
1 tablespoon salt	1 tablespoon flour
2 medium onions, finely diced	1 tablespoon sugar

Combine the first six ingredients and marinate the trout for half an hour. Then simmer for fifteen to twenty minutes. When the fish is cooked, remove to a heated plate and add the flour and sugar to the broth. Cook for a few minutes. Strain. Pour the liquid over the fish.

---

*This recipe used by permission of *Gourmet Magazine*.
**This recipe used by permission of *Gourmet Magazine*.

Trout Cooked in Beer Two

Another beer recipe is to fry the trout in batter.

Sift 1 cup flour, 1 tablespoon sweet Hungarian paprika, and 1 teaspoon salt into a bowl containing 1 cup light beer, whisking, and let the batter stand, covered, for at least 1 hour.

Clean and pat dry four 10- to 12-ounce brook trout, sprinkle them inside and out with lemon juice, salt, and pepper, and dredge them in flour. Coat 1 fish with the batter and in a deep fryer fry it in hot deep oil (375° F.) for 4 minutes, or until it is golden. Transfer the fish to a platter lined with paper towels and keep it warm in a preheated very slow oven (200° F.). Prepare and fry the remaining fish, 1 at a time, in the same manner. Serve the fish with *sauce gribiche* and lemon wedges.*

Truite au Bleu (Blue Trout)

Now that you've run the gamut and cooked trout in corn husks, newspaper, and beer are you ready for the exotic? Could you face a blue trout staring right at you? If so, here's a recipe for *Truite au Bleu* (or Blue Trout).

There are two secrets to the success of this delicacy. One is that the fish must be *very* newly caught. Second, you must plunge it *immediately* into boiling court bouillon consisting of three parts water to one part vinegar. For every quart of water, add:

6 peppercorns	**½ bay leaf (or a larger**
1 teaspoon salt	**or smaller part)**
pepper to taste	

Your trout will cook in approximately four minutes and can be served hot with butter or hollandaise, or cold with mayonnaise. The vinegar turns the fish a metallic, garish blue!

Salmon, Steelhead, and Trout in Paper

A sophisticated company dish is fish cooked in parchment paper. With a mixed green salad it makes a delightful luncheon dish. Wrap salmon, steelhead, or trout steaks or fillets individually in

---

*This recipe used by permission of *Gourmet Magazine*.

parchment paper and cook. You can bring these to the table still in their paper. Each package serves one person.

Flatten lightly six 1-inch-thick salmon steaks between sheets of wax paper. Sprinkle the salmon with salt and pepper and put it in a shallow dish. In a bowl combine 1 cup olive oil, 3 tablespoons lemon juice, 3 shallots, minced, and 2 tablespoons minced parsley. Pour the mixture over the salmon and let the salmon marinate at room temperature, turning it occasionally, for 1 hour.

Oil 6 sheets of parchment paper, each large enough to enclose a steak. Transfer 1 steak to each sheet, spoon 1 tablespoon of the marinade over each steak, and fold the paper over the steaks, crimping the edges tightly. Put the steaks on an oiled baking sheet and bake them in a preheated very hot oven (450°F.) for 20 minutes, or until the paper is puffed and golden. Transfer the steaks to a heated platter and slit the papers ½ inch from the crimped edges. Serve the salmon with lemon wedges.*

Fish Soup (for four to five people)

This is a tasty way to use up leftover fish. For this quick first course, gather together the following ingredients:

2 tablespoons margarine or butter	2 cups Veloute sauce:
1 cup milk	3 tablespoons margarine or butter
½ yellow onion, minced	2 cups fish broth or court bouillon
salt and pepper to taste	3 tablespoons flour
nutmeg	1 cup leftover cooked fish
parsley, minced	

In heavy saucepan, bring butter to boil and add onion and milk. Simmer onion until it is soft, for ten to fifteen minutes. Place half of the fish at a time in a blender and puree with half of the onion-milk-butter mixture. Add pureed fish to the remaining milk and the Veloute sauce. Bring to boil and season with salt, pepper, and nutmeg. Add parsley before serving.

---

*This recipe used by permission of *Gourmet Magazine.*

Salmon or Trout Pizza

Here's a way of serving fish that should be popular with old and young!

Make your favorite pizza dough (or use a ready mix) and put it in a pizza pan. Add the following:

2 cups of shredded cooked trout or salmon	**chopped onions**
	½ cup of thinly sliced fresh mushrooms or
1 small can of tomato sauce	**1 small can of sliced mushrooms**
12 oz. of thinly sliced mozzarella cheese	**¼ teaspoon oregano**
½ cup each of thinly sliced olives, finely chopped green pepper, finely	**salt and pepper to taste**
	½ cup of grated Parmesan cheese

Spread the tomato sauce on the dough and lay in layers the mozzarella cheese, flaked salmon or trout, olives, peppers, onion, and mushrooms. Season with oregano, salt, and pepper. Top with Parmesan cheese.

Bake in oven at 450° for 15 or 20 minutes or until it bubbles.

Steelhead or Salmon Kabobs

A novel way of presenting fish from your favorite stream!

1½ lbs. salmon or steelhead steaks
1 medium zucchini
1 dozen fresh mushrooms
1 dozen cherry tomatoes

Remove skin and bones from the fish and cut into sixteen 1½-inch pieces. Alternate fish, zucchini slices, mushrooms, and tomatoes on each of 4 skewers. Brush with lime or lemon butter. Place on grill about 6 inches above the hot coals. Grill for 8 minutes on each side, basting with lime/lemon butter. Continue cooking until fish starts to flake. This takes about 8 minutes on each side.

Lime or Lemon Sauce (serves four)

½ cup melted butter
2 tablespoons of lime or lemon juice
1½ teaspoons of finely chopped onions
1 clove garlic, which

has been pressed
¼ teaspoon of salt
¼ teaspoon of thyme
dash of pepper

Trout, Steelhead, or Salmon Cakes

With the current popularity of fish cakes these should make a tremendous hit!

2½ cups of shredded cooked trout, steelhead, or salmon.
⅓ cup of fresh parsley tops
4 green onions or 3 shallots
3 cups of finely chopped fresh bread crumbs (white or French bread preferred)
2 eggs

2 tablespoons of melted unsalted butter
2 tablespoons mayonnaise
1 tablespoon spicy brown mustard or Dijon mustard
2 tablespoons fresh lemon juice
salt and pepper to taste
½ cup of vegetable oil for sautéing

Combine parsley, onions, or shallots in food processor and chop fine. Add 1½ cups of bread crumbs, the eggs, melted butter, mayonnaise, mustard, and lemon juice.

Mix and then add fish and process briefly. Season to taste. Refrigerate overnite or for at least one-half hour.

Shape mixture into 12 round patties about ⅜ inch thick. Dip in remaining bread crumbs, coating all sides evenly. Let stand for 5 minutes.

Warm oven to 200°F. and line a baking sheet or ovenproof dish with several thicknesses of paper toweling.

Heat ¼ inch vegetable oil in a large sauté pan or heavy skillet over medium high heat. Sauté patties a few at a time, turning once, and cook until golden brown and crisp on each side. (It takes one or 2 minutes per side.) Remove with slotted spatula to paper-lined baking dish or sheet and place in oven to keep warm. Cook remaining patties and add more oil if needed. Serve with tomato sauce or your favorite sauce.

Tomato Sauce

3 tablespoons olive oil	2 tablespoons of shredded fresh basil
1½ cups chopped yellow onion	1 tablespoon minced fresh thyme or a teaspoon of dried thyme
3 minced garlic cloves	
3 lbs. vine-ripened tomatoes (peeled, seeded, and chopped)	1 bay leaf salt and pepper

Heat oil over medium-low heat. Add onions and sauté them until soft (4 minutes). Stir in garlic and cook 1 minute. Add tomatoes, herbs, salt, and pepper and simmer until liquid reduces and sauce is thick (20 minutes). Remove bay leaf and serve over fish cakes.

Armed with ingenuity, imagination, and your favorite cookbook, BE ADVENTURESOME! For leftover fish, consider fish croquettes, fish balls, fish hash, or fish cakes. Or how about the ever-glamorous fish souffle, or fish mousse? There are also tempting recipes for fish stew or fish gumbo. Excellent fish salads are Trout Nicoise or trout or salmon in aspic. On a rainy Sunday morning, how about a trout omelette? Or be very British and start a meal with potted salmon.

If, by some stroke of bad luck, you are fishless, you could stave off starvation with baked skunk or pickled beaver tail. Digger and Montana Costello give an old-time recipe in their publication "Oregon Outdoors," for these unusual and delectable concoctions. After you have caught, cleaned, skinned, and washed your skunk, bake it in an oven with salt and pepper. It will taste like rabbit and have no smell! For a pickled beaver tail, remove the tail from the body. Singe over a flame until the skin curls. Peel off the skin and soak the tail in salt water for two or three hours. Boil until tender in salted water and marinate in vinegar. Chill and serve.

With all these ideas, how can you resist cooking up a storm?

Appendix

Checklists For A Woman Fisherman

General

Two pairs of jeans
Several warm shirts
Several cotton shirts
Hat for sun or rain
Rubber boots or hiking shoes (or
    waders, depending on fishing)
Sneakers or moccasins for cabin
    wear
Fishing vest (or light parka with
    pockets)
Warm jacket
Rain jacket and rain pants
Sweater or quilted vest
Heavy and thin socks
Warm undershirt (optional)
Warm long johns
Underwear
Pajamas or nightgown
Belt

Gloves
Scarves and/or bandannas
Sunglasses
Reading glasses (if worn)
Toilet articles kit
Sports watch (waterproof)
Bug spray
Sunscreen
Matches
Camera and film
Flashlight and extra batteries
Books for light reading
Fishing knife
Kleenex
Grog (enough for both of you and
    your guide)
Sleeping bag (check to see if you
    should bring yours)
Bathing suit

Strictly for Fishing

Waders and wading shoes
Proper assortment of flies and fly
    boxes
Leaders

Rods, lines, and reels
Clippers
Net
Fishing license

Optional

Pocket-sized bird, wildflower, and
tree guides
Woolite
Laundry line
Wire hangers
Bath towel, washcloth, soap

Games: cards, backgammon,
dominoes, etc.
Binoculars
Pencil and notebook
Small sewing kit

Miscellaneous

First-aid manual
Halazone tablets (to purify water)
Scissors (folding)

Precision tweezers (to remove
thorns, splinters, etc.)
Matches

Toilet Kit

Toothpaste and brush
Comb and/or hairbrush
Soap and washcloth
Small, dark towel
Deodorant
Moisturizer (unscented)

Lipstick
Shampoo
Lots of small Kleenex packs
(Remember that scented lotions
attract insects and will
counteract insect repellent)

Medical Kit

Vitamins
Aspirin
Alka Seltzer or Rolaids
Cough drops
Insect repellent
Lotion for insect bites
Sunburn cream (unscented)
Antihistamine
Medicine for any condition you

may be susceptible to (backs,
knees)
A few emergency prescription
drugs that your doctor will give
you before you go into the wilds
Lomotil
First-aid cream and bandaids
Thermometer
Burn lotion

Good to Bring Along

Extra pair of glasses (if you wear
glasses)

Collapsible drinking cup
Small bottle opener, with

corkscrew
Snakebite kit
Plastic bags for packing

Gum and high-energy candy
Scotch tape

List For Rubber Raft Float Trip

Basic

(Keep kit under twenty-five
  pounds)

Waders and wading shoes
Change of clothing for evening
  camp wear
Pants (not wool or corduroy—they
  take too long to dry)
Underwear
Shirts (not sweatshirts—they don't
  dry fast enough)
Suntan lotion, lip-aid, insect
  repellent
Sleeping bag and air mattress
Plastic drop cloth for rain shelter
Sunglasses with secure head strap
Drinking cup, knife, fork, and
  spoon
Tennis shoes to wear on raft when
  swimming (no thongs—they can
  be dangerous)
Several pairs of socks
Towel and washcloth

Bandanna (serves as scarf, towel,
  potholder, or tourniquet, if
  needed)
Light rain jacket
Sweater
Swim suit
Wide-brim hat (with chin strap—
  straw and tennis hats are good.
  They can be kept wet to stay
  cool in hot weather)
Flashlight with fresh batteries
Personal toiletries (bio-degradable
  soap)—toothbrush, tooth paste,
  comb, Kleenex
Extra tennis shoes or hiking boots
Fishing gear and license
Small, zippered, waterproof bag
  for incidental items you will
  need on the raft (sunscreen,
  Chapstick, Kleenex, sunglasses,
  map, book, camera)
Waterproof dirty-clothes sack

Optional

(If you're allowed more weight)

Botanical, zoological, or geological
  equipment
Books
Camera and lots of film (carry in a

waterproof gas mask bag or
  fifty-caliber ammo box to
  protect against wetness)
Change of fresh clothes (to keep in
  car for drive home)

Chess set, backgammon or dominoes, playing cards
Parka
Warm hat
Knife
Musical instrument
Pillow case (stuff with clothes to form a pillow at night

Plastic bags with fasteners (to keep sand out and duffle in order) one for socks, one for undies, one for sweaters, etc.
Extra reading and sunglasses
Writing materials

What To Leave At Home

Radio
Pets
Contact lenses (too difficult to retrieve if a wave washes them into the river)

Essential Clothing And Equipment For Three-Day Backpacking Trip

Good pair of hiking boots with vibram soles that fit well and give good support (your feet will be your transportation)

3 pairs lightweight wool socks (these may be changed often to avoid blisters)

2 pairs heavy-wool outer socks, extra pair shoelaces

Well-fitted pack with waterproof cover

2 long-sleeved blouses, one cotton, one flannel for protection against sun, insects, and underbrush

Sleeveless blouse or halter worn under shirt (remove outer shirt for suntanning)

Hat for protection against sun, wind, and rain (be sure that it is secure against wind and flexible enough to go inside pack when not in use)

Lightweight sweater

Down jacket for minimum weight and maximum warmth

Windbreaker (can double as raingear)

Pair of sturdy, darker-colored long cotton pants

Walking shorts (optional)

Keds or moccasins to wear around camp

Pair of long thermal underpants to wear under jeans if evenings are chilly (also good substitute for pajamas)

Toilet kit—keep light, but don't forget essentials: soap, towel, comb, lipstick (or other lip protection), toilet paper, Kleenex, insect repellent, sunburn lotion (unscented), liniment (for sore muscles), aspirin, snake-bite kit (if going into snake country), and prescription drugs you need (antihistamine for insect bites, etc.), extra pair of glasses (if you wear them)

Down sleeping bag, foam rubber shorty pad, and ground cloth; drinking cup tied onto belt or pack

Mess kit and cooking utensils, matches in waterproof container, flashlight, pocket knife, small candle, and whistle (in case you get separated from group)

Add or subtract to this list according to the length of your trip and the expected temperature changes, but remember to weigh each item before putting it into your pack.

Clothes For Two Weeks At A Mountain Or Northern Fishing Lodge

(with no washing machine and all packed into two medium-sized, waterproof duffles)

2 flannel nightgowns
1 pair warm slipper shoes
2 pairs long insulated underwear
2 cotton shirts
2 wool shirts
2 pairs jeans
2 pairs wool slacks
2 sweaters
2 turtle necks to wear under waders
1 warm-up suit to wear under waders on cold mornings
1 down jacket
1 fishing vest

1 two-piece rain suit
2 fishing hats, one felt and one nylon or cotton
2 scarves
1 pair of chest-high boot waders with suspenders and belt; can be lightweight Red Ball (easy-to-pack) waders with additional wading shoes.
1 pair light shoes for cabin wear
1 cotton pantsuit to wear to and from camp
4 pairs light socks
4 pairs heavy socks
2 pantyhose for under slacks
Panties and bras (which may be washed by hand)
1 pair short, waterproof boots

Checklists For Five-Day Wilderness Pack Trip On Horseback

Clothing

Rainwear (poncho or slicker)
Warm jacket
Riding boots or hiking boots
Light camp shoes (sneakers or moccasins)
Broad-brim hat that will stay on
Sweater (optional)
Blue jeans (two pairs)
Two or three long-sleeved cotton shirts
Warm sleeping garments (pajamas or warm-up suit)
Cotton long johns
Underwear
Socks (light and one heavy)
Gloves
Bathing suit (optional)

Incidentals

Insect repellent
Sun lotion
Soap
Pocket knife (optional)
Toiletries and cosmetics
Drinking cup (collapsible preferred)
Kleenex
Small towel and washcloth
Glasses (sun and reading)
Bandanna
Reading material
Small cotton ditty bag (about eight by twelve inches) to carry incidentals while riding on the trail

Equipment

Sleeping bag
Fishing tackle and license
Camera and film
Flashlight and batteries
Lightweight waders and wading shoes

Fishing Schools

The best way to learn most sports is to get personal instruction from a professional. Because of the timing and sensitive touch required, fly fishing also requires person-to-person instruction. We have listed a number of schools and suggest that you choose one nearest to you—or nearest a place where you'd like to vacation. The following schools were all in operation at the time of publication but since fly-fishing schools have a tendency to appear and disappear, we recommend you check all listings.

Allenberry Resort Inn, P.O. Box 7, Boiling Springs, PA 17007, (717) 258-3211. The Allenberry Inn holds fly-fishing schools from April until November. Classes are from Friday evening until noon Sunday. Men and women attend the schools, which offer classroom and on-stream learning. Individual casting lessons are given.

George Anderson's Yellowstone Angler, P.O. Box 660, Highway 89 South, Livingston, MT 59047, (406) 222-7130. The Yellowstone Angler holds fishing schools for beginners to experts from mid-May to mid-August. They teach on Lake Merrill as well as at Armstrong Spring Creek, Depuy Spring Creek, and the Yellowstone River. Classes are limited to twelve students, with George conducting each class himself, with the help of experts and local guides. Classes are conducted in quiet, comfortable classrooms. Video cameras film each student to improve casting. Casting sessions are on the spring creeks, the lake, or the Yellowstone River. Guest teachers such as Mel Krieger and Dave Whitlock help in the teaching.

L. L. Bean Fly Fishing Schools, Casco Street, Freeport, ME 04033, (207) 865-4761. The L. L. Bean Fly Fishing Schools, developed by Dave Whitlock nearly a decade ago, have become very popular and fill up early. Introductory programs run for three full days and include lunch and a complete L. L. Bean fly-fishing outfit (rod, reel, line, leader, backing, and handbook). These classes are held in Freeport, Maine, for men, women, and children over ten, and run from May through August every weekend. Intermediate and advanced instruction is given outside of Yellowstone Park in Montana and on the Bighorn River in September and October, and at Grand Lake Stream in Maine in July. Enrollment is limited to twelve students. Fishing is both wading and from McKenzie River boats. L. L. Bean also holds schools for bass in Maine, Atlantic salmon in Labrador, and saltwater fly fishing in Belize.

Beckie's Fishing Creek Outfitters, RD 1, Box 310-1, Fairmont Springs Road, Benton, PA 17814, (717) 925-2225. Excellent one-day classes with one-on-one teaching by Barry or Cathy Beck—casting, knot tying, and river experience using nymphs, streamers, and dry flies on wild brown trout. Both Becks are knowledgeable and superb teachers.

Caucci/Nastasi Fly Fishing Schools, R.D. 1, Box 102, Tannersville, PA 18372, (717) 629-2962. Al Caucci and Bob Nastasi, both superb anglers and the authors of several important books, give courses in entomology and casting on the Delaware River.

Creative Sports Enterprises, 1924C Oak Park Blvd., Pleasant Hill, CA 94523, (415) 938-2255. This group, organized by André Puyans, conducts seminars that are extremely comprehensive and cover every aspect of fly fishing. The student-to-instructor ratio is never more than 2 to 1, except during casting and classroom work; this allows this school to work with any level of expertise. Actual classes are limited to eighteen people. Women are especially welcome. Most of the teaching is conducted under actual fishing conditions, in such places as Island Park, Idaho, and instructors include such special guests as Ernest Schwiebert and Steve Rajeff.

The Fly Box, 923 SE 3rd Street, Bend, OR 97702, (503) 388-3330. The Fly Box holds group classes on weekends. Private lessons can be arranged. There is on-stream instruction as well as classroom teaching. The Fly Box holds floating classrooms on the Deschutes River that are often overnight trips.

Green Mountain Fly Fishing School, P.O. Box 1225, Route 100, Stowe, VT 05672. This school, held on the grounds of The Fly Rod Shop, includes entomology, fly selection, and on-stream instruction.

Henry's Fork Anglers, P.O. Box 487, St. Anthony, ID 83445, (208) 558-7525. The school "season" here runs from Memorial Day weekend until October, Sunday through Saturday, with classes for men, women, and children. There are generally two days in the classroom plus casting instruction, a third afternoon of free time, and three days of instruction on the stream with a guide. Mel Krieger is the casting instructor. Fishing is on the Henry's Fork of the Snake River.

Kaufmann's Fly Fishing Expeditions, P.O. Box 23032, Portland, OR 97223, (503) 639-6400. Classes are held from May through October, with evening casting and fly tying—and there is also a weekend school on the Deschutes, from Saturday to Monday afternoon, where Kaufmann's has a cabin in Maupin.

Mel Krieger School of Fly Fishing, 790 27th Avenue, San Francisco, CA 94121, (415) 752-0192. Mel Krieger, the guru of fly casting, holds fishing classes for beginners and advanced students from March on through the summer until the end of September. He not only teaches in California but also in Oregon, Texas, Arizona, Idaho, Colorado, Montana, Pennsylvania, Massachusetts, Canada, and Belize. He holds two-day, three-day, and week-long schools and teaches all aspects of casting, knot tying, reading the water, choice of flies, and the like. Mel's theatrics and enthusiasm make working with him lots of fun. Private lessons are also available.

Bud Lilly's Trout Shop, P.O. Box 698, West Yellowstone, MT 59758, (406) 646-7801. Jim Criner, the new owner of Bud Lilly's, holds one, two, three, five, and seven-day classes for men and women. There is also a special all-woman's class held once a year. The class spends an hour in the classroom and then is on the stream the first day. Schools run from mid-June until late September.

Madison River Fishing Company, P.O. Box 627, 109 Main Street, Ennis, MT 59729, (406) 682-4293. Hold three-day fly-fishing schools in June and July. Each of their three days are spent on a spectacular piece of trout water, such as Depuy Spring Creek near Livingston, the Gallatin River, and nearby Madison. Guides are assigned on a ratio of one to every two or three fishermen each day.

The Orvis Company, Manchester, VT 05254, (802) 362-1300. For fast learning, try the Orvis Fly Fishing School. They claim they can turn anyone into a competent fly fisherman in three days. The emphasis is on casting, knot tying, entomology, and on-stream instruction. Use of correct equipment is stressed. The school provides rods, lines, and leaders for instruction. At graduation, each student receives a diploma and colorful pin. The classes are for men, women, and children; classes are not only held at the main store in Manchester but at Orvis shops throughout the country.

Powell Rod Company, P.O. Box 3966, Chico, CA 95927, (916) 345-3393. The Powell Rod Company uses the "hands on" method of instruction. Classes begin in early May and run through November. Pupils learn to catch fish and are instructed in flies and knots. Most instruction is on a river but there are also seminars. Men, women, and children ten years and above are invited.

River Meadows, Box 347, Wilson, WY 83014, (307) 733-2841. Fly fishing schools for everyone, from June through September.

Sage/Winslow, 7869 NE Day Road, Bainbridge Island, WA 98110,

(206) 842-6608. Instruction runs from March 1 to October 1 each year, with classes nationwide, from Maine to California and in British Columbia, Alberta, and Alaska. Classes are for men, women, and children twelve years old and up. There are flycasting clinics and one-day fly-fishing schools.

Snug Fly Fishing Service, Box 127, Sun Valley, ID 83353. Snug Stores have a unique school in Sun Valley for children called "Catch and Release." It runs during the summer months and teaches the young to cast, tie knots with foot-long hooks and rope, and sends them home with a Polaroid of their catch. Schools for men, women, and children run from June through September.

Sunnybrook Fly Fishing School, 1104 Fremont Avenue, Sandusky, OH 44870 (419) 625-8353. Fly-casting champion Marion Garber gives personalized instruction.

Take It Easy Fly Fishing Resort, P.O. Box 408-A, Ft. Klamath, OR 97626, (503) 381-2328. The school here, run by Orvis, is given from May through September. Beginner schools run for four days each and are open to both men and women. Pupils are taught technique, basic fly-fishing skills, casting, and on-stream strategies.

Joan and Lee Wulff Fishing School, Box 16, Beaverkill Road, Lew Beach, NY 12753, (914) 439-3798. Joan and Lee Wulff's school consists of two-day weekend schools with theory and practice casting sessions on the Beaverkill. There are courses on entomology, knot tying, flies, reading the water, and the like. The school runs from the spring through the fall. Joan, a champion caster, teaches all ages with great energy and creativity. Video tapes of each student casting are shown to the pupils. The Wulffs also offer a special course in Atlantic salmon fishing. Lee Wulff, a world-famous angler, also teaches students.

In all these schools, pupils are taught to think out a fishing situation they might eventually come up against. The schools vary in their techniques and their offerings. Choose your school according to what you want to learn. Use the phone to find out where you can learn the most. With proper training, you will soon qualify for L. A. Anderson's definition of a successful fisherman: "One can develop," he promises in *Hunting and Fishing and Camping,* "into a successful fisherman if (you) can find where the fish are, tempt them with the right lures and hook and land them properly."

Conservation Organizations

Conservation groups keep appearing all over the United States. These organizations have been helpful in preserving our wilderness areas, our wildlife, and our fish. Such groups as the National Wildlife Federation, with its 3,500,000 members, and the Sierra Club, with its 164,000 members, have proven influential and forceful in bringing about political legislation. Trout Unlimited is the best known of the fish conservation groups. All these organizations are ecology minded, and they depend on public support to survive.

Here is a list of the most important groups. We urge you to join one or more of these organizations, give them financial assistance, and—if you have time—take part in their activities.

American Medical Fly Fishing
  Association
7130 Morningside
Loomis, California 95650

American Museum of Fly Fishing
Manchester, Vermont 05254

American Rivers Conservation
  Council
317 Pennsylvania Avenue, S.E.
Washington, D.C. 20003

Atlantic Salmon Federation
1434 St. Catherine Street W.
Montreal, Quebec
Canada H3G 1R4

British Columbia Steelhead Society
P.O. Box 33947, Station D
Vancouver, British Columbia
Canada V6J 3J3

California Fisheries Restoration
  Foundation
1212 Broadway
Oakland, California 94612

California Trout Inc.
P.O. Box 2046
San Francisco, California 94126

Defenders of Wildlife
2000 "N" Street, N.W.
Washington, D.C. 20036

Environmental Defense Fund
2728 Durant
Berkeley, California 94704

The Environmental Planning
  Lobby
502 Park Avenue
New York, New York 10022

Environmental Policy Center
317 Pennsylvania Avenue SE
Washington, D.C. 20003

The Federation of Fly Fishers
P.O. Box 1088
West Yellowstone, Montana 59758

Foundation for Montana Trout
P.O. Box 652
Ennis, Montana 59729

Friends of the Earth
529 Commercial Street
San Francisco, California 94111

Friends of the Wilderness
3515 East Fourth Street
Duluth, Minnesota 55804

International Game Fish Association
3000 East Las Olas Boulevard
Fort Lauderdale, Florida 33316

Isaak Walton League
1800 North Kent Street, Suite 806
Arlington, Virginia 22209

Michigan United Conservation Club
P.O. Box 2235
Lansing, Michigan 48911

National Audubon Society
950 Third Avenue
New York, New York 10022

National Wildlife Federation
1412 Sixth Street, N.W.
Washington, D.C. 20036

The Nature Conservancy
P.O. Box 258
Helena, Montana 59624

Restoration of Atlantic Salmon in America, Inc.
Box 164
Hancock, New Hampshire 03449

Sierra Club
530 Bush Street
San Francisco, California 94108

Theodore Gordon Flyfishers
24 East 39th Street
New York, New York 10016

Trout Unlimited
(see your local chapter)
Main National Office
P.O. Box 1944
Washington, D.C. 20013

Wilderness Society
1901 Pennsylvania Avenue, N.W.
Washington, D.C. 20006

Wildlife Society
3900 Wisconsin Avenue, N.W., Suite 5176
Washington, D.C. 20016

World Wildlife Fund
1255 23rd Street NW
Washington, DC 20037

Suggested Reading

The literature of fly fishing is vast and we make no attempt to account for even a modest portion of it. But reading about fishing can be lots of fun, and it can be helpful. Here are some books to get you started.

General

Bates, Joseph D., Jr. *Atlantic Salmon Flies and Fishing.*
Brooks, Joe. *The Complete Book of Fly Fishing.*
Camp, Raymond. *The Fireside Book of Fishing.*
Chatham, Russell. *The Angler's Coast.*
Fennelly, John F. *Steelhead Paradise.*
Gierach, John, *Trout Bum.*
Gingrich, Arnold. *The Fishing in Print* and *The Well-Tempered Angler.*
Hackle, Sparse Grey. *Fishless Days, Angling Nights.*
Haig-Brown, Roderick L. *A River Never Sleeps* and *Return to the River.*
Lyons, Nick. *Fisherman's Bounty* (ed.) and *Fishing Widows.*
Maclean, Norman. *A River Runs Through It.*
McDonald, John. *The Origins of Angling* (contains Dame Juliana's Treatise) and *Quill Gordon.*
McClane, A. J. *McClane's New Standard Fishing Encyclopedia.*
Ritz, Charles. *A Fly-Fisher's Life.*
Schwiebert, Ernest. *Trout.*
Scott, Jock. *Greased Line Fishing for Salmon.*
Schullery, Paul. *American Fly Fishing: A History.*
Traver, Robert. *Anatomy of a Fisherman, Trout Madness,* and *Trout Magic.*
Van Fleet, Clark C. *Steelhead to a Fly.*
Walden, Howard T., 2d. *Big Stony* and *Upstream and Down.*
Wulff, Lee. *The Atlantic Salmon.*

Instruction

Bates, Joseph D., Jr. *How to Find Fish—and Make Them Strike.*

Brooks, Charles E. *The Trout and the Stream.*
Brooks, Joe. *Trout Fishing.*
Chatham, Russell. *Striped Bass on the Fly.*
Cordes, Ron. *Flyfishing for Backpackers.*
Fletcher, Colin. *The Complete Walker.*
Gordon, Sid. *How to Fish from Top to Bottom.*
Haig-Brown, Roderick L. *A Primer of Fly Fishing.*
Hayden, Mike. *Fishing the California Wilderness.*
Humphreys, Joe. *Joe Humphreys' Trout Tactics.*
Kreh, Lefty. *Fly Fishing in Salt Water.*
Kreh, Lefty, and Mark Sosin. *Practical Fishing Knots.*
Krieger, Mel. *The Essence of Fly Casting.*
McClane, A. J. *The Practical Fly Fisherman.*
Munz, Philip A. *Handbook on Western Wildflowers.*
Nichols, Maggie. *Wild, Wild Woman.*
Niehaus, Theodore. *Sierra Wildflowers, Mt. Lassen to Kern Canyon.*
Proper, Datus. *What the Trout Said.*
Rosenbauer, Tom. *The Orvis Fly Fishing Guide* and *Reading Trout Streams.*
Thomas, Diane. *Roughing it Easy.*
Whitlock, Dave. *L. L. Bean Fly Fishing Handbook.*
Wulff, Joan. *Joan Wulff's Fly Casting Techniques.*

Fish

Caras, Roger. *Sockeye.*
Combs, Trey. *Steelhead Fly Fishing and Flies* and *The Steelhead Trout.*
Curtis, Brian. *The Life Story of the Fish.*
Jordan, David Starr and Barton W. Evermann. *American Food and Game Fishes.*
McClane, A. J. *Field Guide to Freshwater Game Fishes of North America.*
Moyle, Peter B. *Inland Fishes of California.*
Netboy, Anthony. *The Salmon—Their Fight for Survival.*
Smith, Robert H. *Native Trout of North America.*

Streams

Bardach, John. *Downstream.*
Brooks, Charles E. *The Living River* and *The Henry's Fork.*
Jenkinson, Michael. *Wild Rivers of North America.*
Needham, Paul. *Trout Streams.*

Dry-Fly Fishing

Atherton, John. *The Fly and the Fish.*
Goddard, John, and Brian Clarke. *The Trout and the Fly.*
Halford, F. M. *Dry-fly Fishing in Theory and Practice.*
LaBranche, G. M. L. *The Dry Fly and Fast Water.*
Marinaro, Vincent C. *A Modern Dry-Fly Code* and *In the Ring of the Rise.*

Nymphs and Wet Flies

Brooks, Charles E. *Nymph Fishing for Larger Trout.*
Quick, Jim. *Fishing the Nymph.*
Rosborough, E. H. *Tying and Fishing the Fuzzy Nymphs.*
Schwiebert, Ernest W. *Nymphs.*
Skues, G. E. M. *Nymph Fishing for Chalkstream Trout* and *Minor Tactics of the Chalk Stream.*

Entomology and Fly Tying

Arbona, Fred. *Mayflies, the Angler, and the Trout.*
Boyle, Robert H. and Dave Whitlock. *The Fly-Tyer's Almanac.*
Dennis, Jack. *Handbook of Western Fly Tying.*
Dunham, Judith. *The Art of the Trout Fly.*
Flick, Art. *Art Flick's New Streamside Guide to Naturals and Their Imitations.*
Flick, Art (ed). *Art Flick's Master Fly-Tying Guide.*
Harris, J. R. *An Angler's Entomology.*
McCafferty, W. Patrick. *Aquatic Entomology.*
Schwiebert, Ernest W. *Matching the Hatch.*
Swisher, Doug, and Carl Richards. *Selective Trout.*
Talleur, Richard. *The Fly-Tyer's Primer.*
Whitlock, Dave. *Dave Whitlock's Guide to Aquatic Trout Foods.*

Periodicals

Fly Fisherman. John Randolph, editor and publisher. Fine, well-written articles concerning all types of fly fishing.
Gray's Sporting Journal. Edward E. Gray, editor and publisher. Beautiful magazine with handsome photographs and fine articles on fishing and hunting.
Flyfishing. Frank W. Amato, editor, Portland, Oregon. Interesting coverage

of western fly fishing.

The Flyfisher. Official publication of the Federation of Fly Fishers. A very fine magazine—makes joining this conversation group a double pleasure.

The American Fly Fisher. Journal of the American Museum of Fly Fishing.

The Creel. The well-written bulletin of the Flyfisher's Club of Oregon.

Trout. Official publication of Trout Unlimited. Beautiful periodical. News about preservation of wild fish and wild rivers. Comes with membership in Trout Unlimited.

Random Casts. All the good fishing writers contribute to this fine booklet, which is the official publication of the Theodore Gordon Flyfishers, Inc.

Angler. A western publication, covering all types of fishing.

The Salmon and Trout Magazine. Journal of the English Salmon and Trout Association. Interesting articles on conservation and fishing in English lakes and rivers.

The Sierra Club Bulletin. Good lists of trips available to western fishermen. All kinds of wilderness information. A good reason for joining the Sierra Club.

Outdoor Life. A magazine for all outdoor sports.

Field & Stream. Specializes in hunting and fishing.

Sports Afield. Primarily the field sports, a popular magazine.

Sports Illustrated. Not a lot of fishing articles, but excellent when they do appear.

Fly Rod and Reel: The Journal of American Fly Fishing. An excellent magazine, edited by Silvio Calabi, with fine book reviews, excellent writers, and always a few surprises.

American Angler and Fly Tyer. In-depth coverage of what's new in fly tying—and what's enduring from the past. The new editor and publisher, Dick Stewart, has done a splendid job.